Patrick County, Virginia Unrecorded Documents

1791-1920

Barbara C. Baughan
and
Betty A. Pilson

> The riders in the yard will say the clock stopped
> and ride off laughing into another century.
> Think of us, please.
>
> There will be no one to explain why we forgot the items we left.
> We will appear odd, yet there was possibly a reason.
> We were like you.
> Remember us. This is all that is left.

HERITAGE BOOKS
2008

HERITAGE BOOKS
AN IMPRINT OF HERITAGE BOOKS, INC.

Books, CDs, and more—Worldwide

For our listing of thousands of titles see our website
at
www.HeritageBooks.com

Published 2008 by
HERITAGE BOOKS, INC.
Publishing Division
100 Railroad Ave. #104
Westminster, Maryland 21157

Copyright © 1998 Barbara C. Baughan and Betty A. Pilson

Other books by the authors:
Miscellaneous Records of Patrick County, Virginia
Patrick County, Virginia 1880 Census
Patrick County, Virginia Birth Records: 1853–1869, Volume I
Patrick County, Virginia Birth Records: 1870–1880, Volume II
Patrick County, Virginia Birth Records: 1881–1889, Volume III
Patrick County, Virginia Birth Records: 1890–1896, Volume IV
Patrick County, Virginia Death Records: 1868, 1869, and 1871–1896
Patrick County, Virginia Land Entry Book: July 1791–February 1796
Patrick County, Virginia Superior Court Order Book: May 1809–May 1831
Patrick County, Virginia Will Book, No. 2

All rights reserved. No part of this book may be reproduced or transmitted in any form or by any means, electronic or mechanical, including photocopying, recording or by any information storage and retrieval system without written permission from the author, except for the inclusion of brief quotations in a review.

International Standard Book Numbers
Paperbound: 978-1-58549-011-0
Clothbound: 978-0-7884-7255-8

INTRODUCTION

The abstractions contained in this book were taken from a box of unrecorded documents in the Patrick County Clerk's Office. For various reasons, non-payment of recording fees, lack of proper proof by witness, etc., these documents were never admitted to record. These documents include wills, deeds, agreements, and other assorted instruments, and some of them contain information which cannot be found in other records.

Since these documents are <u>unrecorded</u>, they are not public records. There will be absolutely no public access to these documents, and no requests for copies will be honored. Therefore, we ask that you do not request copies from the Clerk's Office. We have abstracted their language and spellings, and therefore we suggest that you check all possible spellings of your family name when looking for your ancestors.

We have copied the records from the year 1791 through the year 1920. We also want to thank Susan C. Gasperini, Clerk of the Circuit Court of Patrick County, without whose permission we would not have been able to complete this project.

Betty A. Pilson
P. O. Box 742
Stuart, Virginia 24171

Barbara C. Baughan
216 Glenwood Terrace
Stuart, Virginia 24171

THOMAS AYERS

This Indenture made the 18th day of August in the year of our Lord one thousand Eight hundred and twenty five between Thomas Ayers of Patrick and John Jones of the County aforesaid of the other part witnesseth that the said Thomas Ayers for and in Consideration of the sum of one hundred & five dollars to him in hand paid the receipt of which he doth hereby acknowledge hath bargained sold and doth by these presents bargain sell and convey unto the said John Jones one tract of Land lying and being in the County aforesaid and State above mentioned on the East branches of the south Mayo river Called the Roundabout and bounded as follows To wit beginning at a red oak thence Running N°34 W 23 po' to a red oak & S 4 E 56 po' to a black oak N 84 E 54 po' to a post Oak & S 89 E 38 po' crossing a creek to a white oak S 46 E 347 po' to a Chestnut S 20 W 22 po' to a red oak thence a new line S 56 west to the beginning Containing Eighty three acres one third acres more or Less with all the appurtenances there unto belonging as mentioned in a State survey as Letter were all the improvement thereunto retaining to him the said John Jones and his heirs for Ever to be his lawful possession purchased and the said Thos Ayers doth for himself & his heirs warrant and defend the right and title of the said Land from Every person or persons whatEver to him the said John Jones his heirs &c In witness whereof the said Thomas Ayers hath hereunto set his hand and seal the day and year above written

6 Witness
David Hall Jr
+ David Hall Sr

Thos Ayers (seal)

Articles of Agreement dated August 21, 1834, between JOHN D. CLAY and LEMUEL S. CLAY of Floyd County, and OBADIAH TATE, WILLIAM H. TATE and CHARLES S. TATE of Bedford County. Clays sold to Tates 820 acres patented to JOHN CLAY on Greasy Creek with the exception of 100 acres on which MIDDLETON CLAY now resides and 14 and a fraction acres sold to T.M.C. McCABE on the road near the crossing of Greasy Creek and also 108 acres the heirs of JAMES CALLAWAY, deceased, may obtain somewhere on said tract. Consideration $1,200 to be paid in installments. JOHN D. CLAY, LEMUEL S. CLAY, OBADIAH TATE, WILLIAM TATE, CHARLES S. TATE. Teste: THOMAS McCABE.

Deed of trust dated October 18, 1842 between DANIEL PRICE of Patrick County and THOMAS J. PENN, GREENVILLE PENN and PETER P. PENN, Trustee, to secure a debt of DANIEL PRICE in the sum of $124.77 to THOMAS I. PENN, and further to secure a debt of DANIEL PRICE and his father, SAMUEL PRICE, in the sum of $84.94; and a debt to GREENVILLE PENN in the amount of $35.00 by a joint bond with GEORGE PRICE; and to GREENVILLE PENN in the sum of $31.50. Security given to secure the debts, one Negro girl LIZZIE about 17 or 18 years old with her increase, 1 sorrell mare, 2 feather beds and furniture, 1 black and white steer, 8 or 9 hogs, crop of tobacco and corn, household and kitchen furniture and plantation tools. DANIEL (X) PRICE, THOMAS J. PENN & CO., GREENVILLE PENN, P. P. PENN. Witness: GEORGE W. PENN, RICHARD H. SCALES, LEONARD AYERS.

Deed dated January 24, 1848 from JAMES CLARK to WILLIAM M. ABBINGTON, JOHN PRUNTY, JACKSON PENN, JOSEPH KENNERLY, HARRISON C. FRANCE, CLARK PENN and GEORGE C. DODSON, Trustees, for $1.00 doth grant 1-3/4 acre adjoining HENRY KOGER'S line to said trustees or their successors for the free use of a church known as MOUNT PLEASANT CHURCH to the ministers of METHODIST EPISCOPAL CHURCH, south, for the worship of God. JAMES (X) CLARK, WILLIAM M. ABBINGTON, GEORGE C. DODSON, JACKSON PENN, JOSEPH KENNERLY, JR., H. C. FRANCES, CLARK PENN, JOHN PRUNTY. Witness: ROBERT T. MATTHEWS, MIDDLETON W. KOGER, JOSHUA MURROW.

Deed dated December 10, 1843, from GREENVILLE WILLIS, heir of JOSEPH WILLIS, deceased, SAMUEL THOMAS and FEBY THOMAS, his wife, formerly FEBY WILLIS; JOHN WILLIAMSON SMITH, son of THORNTON SMITH, deceased, who intermarried with ELIZABETH WILLIS who is also deceased, to JOHN WILLIS, all of Patrick County. In consideration of $25.00 to GREENVILLE WILLIS and the like sum to JOHN WILLIAMSON SMITH and $30.00 to SAMUEL THOMAS paid by the said JOHN WILLIS, to convey all of their undivided interest in the lands of which JOHN WILLIS died seized, it being 1/10 part each of 394 acres lying on the headwaters of Johnson's Creek. GREENVILLE WILLIS, JOHN W. SMITH, SAMUEL (X) THOMAS, PHEBEA (X) THOMAS. Witness: ZADOCK HALL, AARON McMILLIAN, WILLIAM (X) MARSHALL.

Agreement dated January 6, 1880 from A. A. SHELTON to S. G. RUCKER as follows: " I have this day sold to S. G. RUCKER my Vest place on Rhoda's Creek for which he is to pay me 35 lbs. if I get POLLY VEST'S right and if not 30 lbs. And I give him posession as of this date." A. A. SHELTON. Teste: HAMON C. SHELTON.

Commonwealth of Virginia, Patrick County, to-wit: To W. F. B. TAYLER, E. F. ROBERTSON and JOHN T. AGEE, freeholders of said county. For as much as E. R. STEPHENS has given information to me, J. T. WEST, a Justice of said county that he did on October 15, 1879 on his land take up an estray jackass, you are hereby commanded (after you have been served) to well and truly view and appraise the said jackass and certify as to the value and description. J. T. WEST, Justice of the Peace.

To the Clerk of the County Court, We, W.F.B. TAYLER, E. F. ROBERTSON and JOHN T. AGEE, 3 freeholders do certify that we have appraised a jackass taken up by E. R. STEPHENS and assess the value at $18.33-1/3. The said jackass is bluish gray, height about 4 feet, age about 8 years. Dated January 6, 1880. W. F.B. TAYLER, E. F. ROBERTSON, J. T. AGEE.

Deed dated June ____, 1870, from SAMUEL G. STAPLES and CAROLINE H. STAPLES, his wife, to CHARLES M. SHELTON (son of LEE SHELTON). In consideration of $130.00 Staples do grant 13 acres on waters of South Mayo River. SAMUEL G. STAPLES. (No signature of wife or relinquishment of dower.)

Dower of JULIA CARTER, widow of BANES CARTER, deceased. Pursuant to an order made at June term of said Court 1868, the undersigned report that they went upon the land named in the order on the 9th day of July, 1868, and assigned to the widow the following boundary of the said 293 acres, beginning at a chestnut tree on the north side of the wagon road near LEWIS PARKER'S, the road being the line; thence a north course to a poplar near MRS. DODSON's spring; thence down the spring branch to HOLLANDSWORTH'S line; thence west with JAMES INGRAM'S new survey to a maple on the falling branch in JAMES VIA'S line; thence his line south to the wagon road; thence with the road to the beginning, including the sulphur spring now owned by WILLIAM TINNEY. ELIJAH PEDIGO, JAMES P. (X) MARTIN, OBADIAH TURNER, JOSEPH M. STOVALL.

Deed of trust dated May 29, 1864 between DIDA MAY of the first part, GEORGE W. MITCHELL of the second part, and JOHN A. FLOYD of the third part, to secure a debt of DIDA MAY in the sum of $53.82 due GEORGE W. MITCHELL. Security given, one bay horse, one red cow, 2 yearlings, 14 hogs, 4 sheep, said DIDA MAY to posses and injoy the use of said secured property unless default be made in payment. DIDA (X) her mark MAY. Witness: WILLIAM P. FLOYD. (On the back of the document was written "10 miles west of Courthouse, 50 cents per acre, no buildings.)

Deed of Homestead dated November 19, 1870 by JORDAN KEATON, a householder and head of a family, intends to avail himself of the homestead, exempt from levy, seizure, garnisheeing and sale, doth declare the following property: home tract on Matthews Creek adjoining poorhouse land, JAMES A. HARBOUR, SALLY FULCHER and others 88 acres - $264.00; 54 acres on headwaters of Matthews Creek on the southeast face of Bull Mountain adjoining SALLY FULCHER and others - $54.00; the purchase money due from THOMAS SHELTON for a tract of land sold under decree of Circuit Court in the case of MAT KEATON v. JORDAN KEATON - $90.00; various items of personal property including farm animals and farm tools, and crops for an aggregate value of $633.75. Oath made before HENRY YOUNG, J. P. Teste: L. G. RUCKER, Clerk.

Deed dated June 18, 1870 between SAMUEL G. STAPLES and CAROLINE STAPLES, his wife, to JAMES TUGGLE. Consideration of $250.00 for 25 acres by survey on South Mayo River. SAMUEL G. STAPLES (No signature for wife or relinquishment of dower).

Patrick County Court on October 25, 1869. This day came WILLIAM M. FRANCIS who alleges that he is aggrieved by an entry in the land book made by WILLIAM I. CRADDOCK, Commissioner of the Revenue in District No. 1 for the year 1869, whereby he is charged $3.64 taxes on two tracts of land on Dan River, 1 containing 135 acres and the other 179 acres. Thereupon he moved the Court to exonerate him from the payment of said taxes erroneously charged, which motion was defended by GEORGE W. BOOKER, Attorney for the Commonwealth. Witnesses were called, G. F. SMITH, Surveyor of the county, and it appearing that the 2 tracts were recovered from the said Francis by BEVERLY A. DAVIS several years ago by being embraced in a large survey, the said Francis is exonerated. Teste: L. G. RUCKER, Clerk.

Deed of Trust dated December 16, 1872 between ARCH S. NOWLIN and J. T. (?). Security: 2 black horses and 2 horse waggons, 1 yoke of oxen and harness for said horses, for debts in the amount of $190.00 to THOMAS D. (?) and $112.50 to W. D. BRAMMER. A.S. NOWLIN.

Deed dated November 7, 1836 between GREENVILLE W. PENN and HENRIETTA M. PENN, his wife, to CLARK PENN. Consideration $80.00 for conveyance of all their right, title and interest to all the undivided land of GABRIEL PENN, deceased, which was allotted to JANE PENN, widow, as a dower, containing 408 acres with all appurtenances. GREENVILLE W. PENN, HENRIETTA M. PENN. Witness: MUNFORD SMITH. A.M. SMITH, SUSAN H. SMITH. WILLIAM CRITZ and THOMAS J. TATUM, Justices of the Peace, acknowledged relinquishment of dower of Henrietta.

Deed dated October 18, 1828 from JESSE DEHEART to WILLIAM LEE. Consideration of $80.00 conveys 40 acres on Joint Crack Creek, adjoining STEPHEN HUBBARD'S line. JESSE DEHART. Witness: THOMAS (X) TENISON, ELIJAH DEHART, JAMES DEHART, STEPHEN HUBBARD.

Indenture dated August 7, 1833, between JOHN STOARD and his children, WILLIAM C. STOARD, GEORGE L. STOARD, MARY J. STOARD, and SUZANNER STOARD and CHARLES FOSTER, JR.
Witnesseth that the said children voluntarily and with the approbation of the said JOHN STOARD, hath put, place and bound themselves to be apprentices with CHARLES FOSTER and as apprentices

with him to dwell till the said children shall attain the age of 21 years which will be on October 9, 1842, September 10, 1843, September 15, 1846, and December 10, 1848, during such time to faithfully serve him in all lawful business and honestly and obediently behave themselves towards the said Foster and his family. The said Foster will instruct the children in the art and mystery of a blacksmith, carpenter, and seamstress and to make the said children as perfect in said arts as possible, and will allow said children good and sufficient meat, drink, apparel, washing, and lodging during said term. JOHN (x) STOARD, CHARLES FOSTER, JR. Teste: DAVID PHILPOTT, JOHN (X) CONNER, LABOURN (X) THURMOND.

Deed dated September 6, 1824 between BARTLEY GREENWOOD and NANCY GREENWOOD, his wife, to ELIJAH EDWARDS. Consideration of $68.00 do convey a parcel of land on Lovings Creek and part of the land sold to BARTLEY GREENWOOD by ELKANAH AYERS. BARTLEY GREENWOOD. Witness: WILLIAM P. AYERS, M.C. (X) her mark GREENWOOD, ELIZABETH (X) GREENWOOD.

Deed of trust dated September 8, 1886 between JOHN HOWELL and JNO R. MOORE, Trustee. Security - all of his right, title and interest, being 1/4, of the tract of land of which MARK W. HOWELL died seized, also one other fourth being the interest of MRS. E. J. HOWELL, wife of MARK HOWELL, of Ohio. This deed conveys the interest in his and Mrs. Howell's revision after the widow's dower, to secure J. J. COLLINS $250.00. JOHN HOWELL.

Deed dated May 9, 1803 between MESHECK BARROTT of Stokes County, North Carolina, and SAMUEL STAPLES. Consideration of $40.00 conveys a tract of land containing 50 acres. MESHECK (X) BARROTT. Attest: ISAAC DODSON, JOHN PATTERSON, DANIEL (X) FAIN.

Deed of Homestead dated December 17, 1870 by ABRAM J. SPENCER, a householder and head of a family, intending to avail himself of a homestead exempt from levy, seizure, garnisheeing or sale doth declare the following: 127 acres on North Mayo adjoining LEWIS SPENCER and other - $381.00; Land bought of ROBERT WILLIAMS containing 100 acres - $300, only $200 paid; Tract containing 180 acres bought at the sale of EZECHIAL PURDY, deceased - $187.00, only $100.00 paid; various items of personal property and farm animals and tools - ABRAM SPENCER.

Note - $161.25 dated April 28, 1882. On or before December 1, 1882, I promise to pay JAMES E. TILLEY the inst sum, waiving the benefit of homestead. A. M. DURHAM. Teste: J. C. SCALES.
For the punctual payment thereof I bind my entire crop of corn and tobacco and wheat raised on J. E. TILLEY'S land in Dan River Township. A. M. DURHAM.

Deed of Homestead dated December 21, 1887 by PETER M. DILLON, householder and head of a family, intending to avail himself of a homestead, exempt from levy, seizure, garnisheeing, or sale, doth declare the following: No real estate whatsoever; 4 hogs marked with a smooth cross in 1 ear - $8.00; 1 white cow and 1 white calf

4

- $25/00; household and kitchen furniture - $15.00; all debts due him - $80.00; Aggregate value $158.00. PETER M. DILLON, Sworn to before BEN J. CAMPBELL, Commissioner in Chancery.

Deed dated October ___, 1859, between WILLIAM AYERS and LUCINDA AYERS, his wife, to WILLIAM MARTIN. Consideration $300.00 conveys 97 acres on south fork of North Mayo River adjoining JAMES TAYLOR. (Not signed)

Deed of trust dated April 8, 1805 between SAMUEL STRONG and BRETT STOVALL. That the said SAMUEL STRONG in order to secure payment of the following debts: 1 debt due SAMUEL MYERS and SOLOMON MYERS, assignees of ROWAN & SCOTT in the amount of 10 pounds and 5 shillings; SAMUEL PANNEL, Executor of DAVID PANNEL, deceased, 13 pounds and 4 shillings; SCALES ADAM & CO. 10 pounds and 2 shillings. Security - tract of land on Bull Mountain fork of South Mayo River adjoining ELIPHAZ SHELTON and GEORGE CARTER, SR. containing 198 acres by survey (being the land conveyed from JACOB CRITZ). SAML STRONG, BRETT STOVALL. Witness: ELIJAH BANKS, GAB. PENN, D. BANKS, SR.

Deed dated August 11, 1825 from THOMAS AYERS to JOHN JONES. Consideration $105.00 conveys 83-1/3 acres on the east branches of the South Mayo River called the Roundabout. THOMAS AYERS Witness: DAVID HALL, JR., DAVID HALL, SR.

Deed dated March 20, 1835 from ROBERT HAYNES and JOSHUA HAYNES of Highland County, Ohio, heirs of JOSHUA HAYNES, SR. to RICHARD HAYNES. Consideration $100.00 convey all their right, title and interest in the Estate of JOSHUA HAYNES, SR. which vests in us by a certain deed of gift executed by JOSHUA HAYNES and recorded in the Clerk's Office of the County of Patrick. ROBERT (X) HAYNES, JOSHUA (X) HAYNES, ZACHARI (X) MORRIS, CLARSSIA (X) MORRIS (No explanation for these 2 signatures). Witness: ALEXANDER HAYNES, THOMAS SNOW, JOSHUA HAYNES, JR.

Agreement dated August 28, 1879, between MATILDA GILBERT, the mother of ADINA GILBERT and WILLIAM A. GILBERT, infants under the age of 14 years, and WILLIAM A. BURWELL.
By consent of the County Court, the said MATILDA GILBERT has placed the said ADINA GILBERT, age 8 years on August 8, 1879 and WILLIAM A. GILBERT, age 6 years on April 7, 1878, apprentices to the said Burwell until Adina shall become 18 years old and William 21 years old; and that the said children shall serve him faithfully in all lawful business and the said Burwell shall teach and instruct Adina in the art and mystery of housekeeping, cooking, washing, and all domestic duties, and William in the art and mystery of farming, and shall teach them reading, writing and common arithmetic, and shall provide sufficient meat, drink, apparel, lodging, and washing. MATILDA GILBERT. WILLIAM A. BURWELL. Witness: THOMAS (X) GILBERT.

Deed of trust dated February 15, 1901 between TAZEWELL M. FAIN and A. E. FAIN, his wife, and RUFUS WOOLWINE, Trustee. Security:

A tract of land containing 82 acres on Mayo River bounded by JOHN HANDY, WILLIAM MARTIN and WILLIAM OVERBY and conveyed to Fains by JEFFERSON HANDY, and the land on which the Fains now reside, to secure E. C. HANKS $750.00. TAZEWELL M. FAIN.

Richmond - April 6, 1886 - This is to inform all whom it may concern that I have annulled and revoked the Power of Attorney heretofore given to A. P. STAPLES, and desire that this paper be entered. WALLER R. STAPLES.

Agreement between WILLIAM C. SMART and JOSEPH MARTIN, _____ MARSH and T. F. GRAVES of Surry County, North Carolina. Consideration $150.00 conveys a tract of land containing 500 acres above Carter's Mill in Carter's Mountain adjoining SILAS CARTER, TIM CAMPBELL, CHARLIE DeHART, MURRY TURNER and RILEY ROBERTSON. Dated September 13, 1875. W. C. (X) SMART.

Inventory of all the property, real and personal, of J. W. HATCHER on which he desires to claim his homestead as against the debt of A. HINES on which debt judgment has been obtained and execution issued, which executions are now in the hands of J. T. W. CLEMENT, Constable. 162 acres on Dan River; 47 acres on Dan River, and various items of personal property and farm animals.

Deed of trust dated May 19, 1877 between JONATHAN C. SANDLIN and JOHN R. MOORE, Trustee. One house and lot in Old Fort, North Carolina. To save harmless A. W. MARTIN in the sale made by him as trustee of 50 acres of land to A. J. DALTON for $200.00. J. C. SANDLIN.

Deed of trust dated January 9, 1900 from J. P. SPENCER to A. RATLIFF, Trustee. Security: 6 hogs, 3 sheep and their increase, 5 bushels corn, 1000 pounds fodder and all crops that I raise this year to secure B.D. CONYWAY $8.40; WILLIAM J. LAW $5.00; and BILLY M. RATLIFF $10.00. J. P. SPENCER.

Deed dated July 2, 1870 between SAMUEL G. STAPLES and CAROLINE STAPLES, his wife, and AARON BLACKARD. Consideration $350.00 conveys a tract of land containing by survey 35 acres on the waters of South Mayo River adjoining JAMES TUGGLE, JOSIAH SHELTON and C.M. SHELTON. SAMUEL G. STAPLES. (Dower of wife not relinquished.)

Deed of trust dated March 29, 1884, between WILLIAM HIATT, HENRY C. CLARK and GEORGE W. HIATT. Whereas WILLIAM HIATT is indebted to GEORGE W. HIATT in the sum of $75.00 and to secure said debt does grant a parcel of land containing 35 acres on Johnson's Creek. WILLIAM HIATT. R. M. CLARK, J.P. notarized deed. (Deed of trust paid in full March 20, 1899.)

Deed dated November 27, 1827 between GEORGE ROGERS of Hawkins County, Tennessee for himself and Attorney in Fact for ANN ROGERS, in connection with JOHN SMITH of Patrick vs. ISHAM SMITH and POLLY SMITH, his wife; MARK SMITH and A.S. CAROLINE SMITH, his wife of the State of Georgia; also MARRY PARR, NATHANIEL SMITH and MARY

SMITH, his wife, BARTHOLOMEW SMITH and DOLLY SMITH, HIS WIFE, JOSIAH S. ELLIS and SUSANNA ELLIS, his wife, all of the State of Tennessee, also HARBARD SMITH and ELIZABETH SMITH, his wife, of the State of Alabama, DANIEL FRANS and SUSANNA FRANS, his wife, of the State of Kentucky, also MUNFORD SMITH of Patrick County, Virginia, for themselves assigned there(?) deed of said land and has been recorded) and ANTHONY OVERBY. Consideration $1,100.00 conveys 760 acres on Peters Creek adjoining GEORGE WASHINGTON GOINS, ANDREW JOYCE. No signatures and no witnesses.

Survey dated April 21, 1883 by M. E. LEWIS, Surveyor for JOHN HURD 24-1/2 acres adjoining F. W. EDWARDS and other in Floyd County.

Shoals, Indiana - July 24, 1876 - L. G. RUCKER, Esq. Please find enclosed a Power of Attorney for part of the heirs of STACY TERRY. MRS. HOPPER is dead, leaving 4 children. 2 of whom are in Missouri. They have no guardian. JACOB C. HOPPER and WILLIAM R. HOPPER reside in Kentucky.

Please forward the money to me at Shoals per Adams Express to deliver on signing of proper vouchers. Please enclose such receipts as you desire to have signed. I will sign it on the sending of the money to the express office at Shoals. THOMAS M. CLARKE.

Know all men by these presents that we, HENRY T. TERRY, JOSEPH P. TERRY, WILSON W. TERRY (JACOB C. TERRY and WILLIAM R. TERRY line out), WYATT J. TERRY, ELKANAH F. TERRY, JOHN W. TERRY, (JAMES HOPPER and ELIZABETH R. HOPPER, his wife, formerly ELIZABETH R. TERRY lined out), and MILAM D. FLETCHER and MINERVA A. FLETCHER, his wife, formerly MINERVA A. TERRY, children and distributees of STACY TERRY, deceased, do appoint THOMAS M. CLARK of Shoals, Indiana, our Attorney in Fact to collect all monies or property due us as heirs of STACY TERRY, deceased, and especially to recover from the Commissioner appointed by the Circuit Court of Patrick County in a chancery cause designated SUSAN VEST v. JOHN HOWELL, et als, the money due us by a decree pronounced in said cause. Dated: July 24, 1876. HENRY T. TERRY, JOSEPH P. TERRY, WILSON (X) TERRY, WYATT J. TERRY, ELEANA T. TERRY, JOHN W. TERRY, MILAM D. FLETCHER, MINERVA A. (X) FLETCHER. Acknowledged in Martin County, Indiana, by EPHRAIM MOSER, Notary Public.

Deed dated May 22, 1905, between E. PARR and AGNES PARR, his wife, and JOHN HURD. In consideration of $20.00 conveys 24-1/2 acres in Floyd County as shown by survey made by M. E. LEWIS March 15, 1883. (No signatures)

Bill of sale dated July 26, 1905 between F. J. CHILDRESS and GEORGE W. CHILDRESS. In consideration of $50.00 conveys one cow black and white spotted, dehorned, about 6 years old; one 1-horse wagon and all growing crops of corn and other products for the year 1905. F. J. CHILDRESS. Notarized by C. R. MARTIN, Clerk.

Plat of survey dated August 25, 1897 for JOHN CRADDOCK as

bought from GEORGE MARTIN containing 61 acres. R. M. CLARK, Surveyor.

Deed dated January 24, 1888 between JOHN RANGELEY and MARIA ANNETTE RANGELEY, his wife; JOHN T. NOEL and MARY NOEL, his wife; and HANNAH AYERS, and WILLIAM DEARMAN. In consideration of $123.75 due by bonds in one, two and three installments, 49-1/2 acres on Dan River adjoining JERRY SMITH. JOHN RANGELEY, MARIA A. RANGELEY, JOHN F. NOEL, HANNAH AYRES (no notarization for last 2 signatures).

Deed dated August 8, 1887 between JOSEPH H. CARTER and JAMES W. CARTER. In consideration of support and maintenance of JOSEPH CARTER and his wife during their natural lives conveys all of their stock, household and kitchen furniture and 67 acres of land on the head waters of Jack's Creek adjoining W. D. BRAMMER and H. T. BRAMMER. JOSEPH H. (X) CARTER

Deed dated September 26, 1875 between PLEASANT NOWLIN of Franklin County and DAVID NOWLIN and his children of Patrick County. In consideration of $300.00 conveys a tract of land on the headwaters of Rock Castle Creek, it being a part of a patent issued to JOHN BURNETT on August 10, 1804, lying west of a branch known as Burnett's Branch, containing 350 acres. PLEASANT NOWLIN. Acknowledged before THOMAS H. HOWARD, Justice of the Peace for Floyd County.

Deed dated January 20, 1827 between JAMES W. McCRAW of Surry County, North Carolina and JACOB KELLAR. In consideration of $200.00 conveys 100 acres of land. JAMES W. McCRAW. Witness: ARCHIBALD STUART, MARTIN CLOUD.

Deed of trust dated July 18, 1866 between HEZEKIAH FAIN and JOHN G. STAPLES, Trustee. Security: one bay mare to secure payment of a note executed to DAVID STUART in the amount of $80.00. HEZEKIAH (X) FAIN. Witness: P. L. YOUNG, JOHN H. CLARK. Acknowledged before WILLIAM C. STAPLES, Notary Public.

Deed of trust dated May 27, 1807 between STEPHEN PAYNE and GREENSVILLE PENN. Whereas JACOB CRITZ hath entered himself as security for STEPHEN PAYNE to GREENSVILLE PENN and THOMAS PENN for a waggon to be delivered to said Penns on or before December 25 next. In order to indemnify the securityship there is conveyed 1 sorrell mare, 1 bay mare and colt, one 1-yr old colt and 8 head of cattle. STEPHEN (X) PAYNE, GREENSVILLE PENN. Witness: JAMES MAY, GEORGE F. CRITZ.

Deed dated September 7, 1839 between THOMAS BROWN and CATY BROWN, his wife, of Stokes County, North Carolina and JAMES PADGETT of Stokes County, North Carolina. In consideration of $1.00 but more particularly for the love, regard and friendship the said Browns have for their son-in-law, conveys 127 acres on the branches of Green Creek bounded by MOLLY BROWN, RICHARD HUDNALL, SR., POWEL GRAY, HARDIN HAIRSTON and JAMES PENN. THOMAS (X) BROWN, CATY (X) BROWN.

Deed dated October 12, 1795 between JACOB CRITZ and MARY CRITZ, his wife, of Patrick County and JOHN MATTHEWS of Amherst County. In consideration of 5 shilling and further consideration of 40 pounds, conveys 200 acres in Amherst County on the waters of Nassaw or Duck Creek adjoining the lands of WILLIAM BARLEY, JOSEPH LANMUM and WILLIAM TURNER, it being the same land which was given to JACOB CRITZ by his father, HAMON CRITZ, by gift, and it being the same land given to HAMAN CRITZ by HAMER and KING. JACOB CRITZ, MARY CRITZ.

Deed dated February 10, 1834 between ELIJAH DAWSON and HARDIN H. MOOR. In consideration of $100.00 conveys 50 acres on a branch of Down Creek lying on both sides of the Virginia road. ELIJAH E. (X) DAWSON Witness: MARTIN CLOUD, ANDREW BRANSON.

I, GEORGE REYNOLDS, hath this day sold and do hereby transfer to THOMAS PENN all my interest and claim in the dower slaves and all other property which my mother holds as widow of JESSE REYNOLDS, deceased. Dated November 15, 1833. GEORGE REYNOLDS. Teste: GREENSVILLE PENN.

I, WILLIAM CARTER, JR. of Stokes County, North Carolina do relinquish all my right to certain negroes given to me in loan by WILLIAM CARTER, SR. for SALLY HANBY, wife of SAMUEL HANBY CHICK. Dated April 1, 1828. WILLIAM CARTER, JR. Attest: POLLY CARTER, MALINDA CARTER, M.D. CARTER.

Deed dated November 13, 1824 between MARTIN BOLT and PARKER HALL. In consideration of $100.00 conveys 150 acres on Johnson's Creek. MARTIN BOLT. Witness: THOMAS SNOW, JAMES (X) PUCKET, THOMAS McMILLION.

Deed of trust dated March 14, 1839 between JAMES L. TAYLOR, GEORGE TAYLOR and GREENSVILLE PENN, Trustee. JAMES L. TAYLOR stands indebted to GEORGE TAYLOR in the sum of $153.00, and to secure said debt conveys the following property as security: 1 bed and furniture; 3 head of cattle; 10 hogs, 1 cupboard and furniture, 1 sorrell horse and plantation tools. JAMES L. TAYLOR, GEORGE D. TAYLOR, GREENSVILLE PENN. Witness: JNO HIGHTOWER, WILLIAM AYERS, THOMAS J. PENN.

Deed of trust dated December 29, 1837 between DANIEL BOOTH and SUSANNAH BOOTH, his wife, and JESSE P. DeHART and THOMAS DeHART. Whereas, Booths are indebted to THOMAS DeHART in the sum of $108.83 by bonds and are desirous of securing said debt, they do hereby convey the following property as security: 1 negro boy named BOOKER. DANIEL BOOTH, SUSANNAH (X) BOOTH, JESSE DeHART, THOMAS DeHART. Witness: AARON DeHART, THAMER (X) her mark ALEXANDER, JOHN ALEXANDER, DANIEL (X) LYON, WILLIAM CANADAY.

Deed of trust dated July 27, 1838 between ALEXANDER AYERS, MARTIN CLOUD and DAVID R. TAYLOR. ALEXANDER AYERS is indebted to DAVID TAYLOR in the sum of $30.68 and conveys the following as security for said debt: Crop of corn now growing, oats, potatoes;

one bed and furniture and all other household furniture, plantation utensils and cross cut saw. ALEXANDER AYRES, MARTIN CLOUD, DAVID R. TAYLOR. Witness: ESOM CLARK, JOHN SCOTT, JAMES DEAN.

Know all men by these presents that I, JOHN RICKMAN, a free man of colour, for the consideration of $2.00 paid by CHRISTOPHER ZEIGLAR and JOHN CASTLE do agree to compromise all law suits now brought and that may be brought in consequence of any disagreements, strikes, assaults, disputes and difficulties that may have heretofore occurred, and I do hereby accord with Zeigler and Castle and compromise all defences of character whatsoever, and I bind myself to dismiss all suits. JOHN (X) RICKMAN. Witness: ROBERT JOHNSON, GEORGE WIGGENGTON, CRAWFORD TURNER.

Deed dated January 18, 1841 between CHARLES FOSTER of Ha__rd County, Georgia and JANE FOSTER of Patrick County, and THOMAS S. SMITH of Franklin County. In consideration of $550.00 conveys 200 acres on the south side of Smith River which was conveyed in trust by LEWIS FOSTER to THOMAS PRILLAMAN to secure a debt due GREENSVILLE FOSTER and sold by Prillaman on December 28, 1840, whereby CHARLES FOSTER became the purchaser, the said JANE FOSTER, the wife of Lewis only holding a dower right, said land adjoining CHARLES SMITH and PACK WOOD. CHARLES FOSTER, JANE FOSTER (mother of Charles). Charles Foster's signature not notarized.

I have sold and delivered to JOHN GILBERT 25 acres of land lying on the west side of Shelton's Creek and above the mill and house in which he now resides. I promise and oblige myself to make said Gilbert a good and lawful deed as soon as the purchase money is paid. November 10, 1840. A. STAPLES.

Deed dated September 21, 1827 between WILLIAM PHILLIPS and WILLIAM EPPERSON. In consideration of $100.00 conveys 85 acres on the south waters of Clark's Creek adjoining BARTLETT SMITH. WILLIAM PHILLIPS. Witness: WILLIAM SMITH, GEORGE SMITH, EWELL SMITH.

Deed dated November 24, 1840 between JAMES W. WAUHOP and JOHN SCOTT. Wauhop sells all of the old tracts of land called the THOMAS AYERS tract, this being the land that Scott has at this time in possession, and it being part of the land sold by JOHN TATUM as Trustee for $200.00. JAMES W. WAUHOP. Witness: ENOS HIATT, MARTIN CLOUD, FRANCIS L. LYON .

Relinquishment by ELENOR FOLEY, one of the heirs of BARTLEY FOLEY, deceased, and have this day sold to HUMPHREY SMITH all and singular my right, title and interest in and to all the lands and tenements which the said Foley died seized of for value received and do hereby relinquish all claims to his estate. Dated December 26, 1796. ELENOR (X) FOLEY. Witness: DAVID HARBOUR, SR., LUKE (X) FOLEY, OLEVIA (X) SMITH.

Deed dated June 6, 1895 between BARBARA FOLEY, SR. and ELIZABETH LAURENCE. In consideration of 6 pounds conveys 20 acres, adjoining JON BURNETT. BARBARY (X) FOLEY, SR., ELIZABETH (X) DEWEZE, MARY (X) FOLEY, RACHAEL (X) FOLEY, BARBARY (X) FOLEY, JR., NANCY (X) FOLEY, BREADGET (X) FOLEY. Witness: JOHN FERRIS, WILLIAM PR BRANHAM, JOHN PR BRANHAM.

Deed dated March 31, 1794 between MICHAEL CLOSE of Pittsylvania County and GEORGE HAIRSTON of Henry County. In consideration of 30 pounds conveys 70 acres on the north side of Mayo, it being part of the land Close purchased from WILLIAM FRENCH and the said French of THOMAS MAN RANDOLPH adjoining HAMON CRITZ. MICHAEL M. CLOSE. Witness: JOSEPH TAYLOR, SAMUEL SHELTON, LEVI METHVIN.

Miss RUTH MURPHY December 23, 1848. In account with PRIOR TATUM, Guardian. Expenses $49.55. By hire of your Negro man CLEM for 1847 - $54.00, cash received for rent oats - $2.00, Balance due $6.45 less commission of $4.20. Balance due RUTH MURPHY $2.25. JOHN G. LEE, GEORGE W. HYLTON, GEORGE PANNILL.

It is agreed between JOSHUA ADAMS and JAMES ADAMS that the said JAMES ADAMS is to have and occupy and manage a tract of land of 87 acres conveyed by MARY BANKS to the said JOSHUA ADAMS as Trustee for THOMAS ADAMS and JAMES W. ADAMS, the ____ of the said JAMES ADAMS for and during the infantcy (or until they attain lawful age) of the aforesaid THOMAS ADAMS and JAMES W. ADAMS, the rents of which are to be annually appropriated to the support and maintenance of the said infants, it be understood however that the said JOSHUA ADAMS reserved to himself the right to resume the possession as soon as he becomes satisfied that profits are not applied in the way directed. September 25, 1849. JOSHUA ADAMS, JAMES ADAMS. Witness: A. STAPLES, M. D. CARTER.

Last Will and Testament of N. D. HILL, SR. To daughter LAURA MARTIN $1.00; personal property sold at public auction and proceeds equally divided among living children with the exception of LAURA MARTIN. ROBERT E. HILL and N. D. HILL, JR. Executors. N D. HILL, SR. Witness: J. J. LEAKE, M.D., J. A. LEAKE.

I, JOSHUA HAYNES, do request that after my death that the County Court give unto my Negro BILL free papers so that he can pass as a free man of coller and that the said BILL can from this time on trade as a free man and that any bargain made by him may be binding. And it is further understood that the said BILL is to live with me and take care of me during my natural life. December 20, 1834. JOSHUA (X) HAYNES. Witness: JAMES W. WAUHOP, S. HAYNES.

Deed of trust dated October 13, 1837 between JOHN B. HUDSON, MILTON R. DODSON and JAMES M. SMITH, Executor of JAMES M. REDD, deceased, in his individual character and as the surviving partner of DAVID H. REYNOLDS & CO. JOHN B. HUDSON is indebted to JAMES M. SMITH, Executor, in the sum of $22.98, and in the sum of $97.94, and $1.00, and $50.96, and doth convey the following to secure said sums: 10 acres on Russell Creek adjoining WILLIAM BOILES and also

JOHN CALLAWAY, it being the same on which the mill is erected. JOHN B. HUDSON, M. R. DODSON, JAMES W. SMITH, Exec. Witness: SEABIRD H. B. COCHRAM, WILLIAM EDWARDS, JOSEPH H. HUDSON.

List of surveys by virtue of land office Treasury Warrants in the year 1882. H. STANLEY and H. MARSHALL - 182 acres; JAMES T. WILLARD - 160 acres; ALEXANDER RATLIFF - 48 acres. M. E. LEWIS, January, 1883.

Deed dated February 1, 1837 between WILLIAM ALLEN, JR., PRESTON ALLEN, ROBERT BRAGEN and GRACEY BRAGEN, his wife, formerly GRACEY ALLEN, of Franklin County and THOMAS KENDRICK of Washington County and ISAAC ADAMS. Whereas, JOHN KENDRICK, SR., deceased, in his lifetime did sell unto THOMAS FLOWERS 393 acres on the water of Buffalo Creek, it being the same land patented in the name of JOHN KENDRICK July 8, 1780. Whereas, the said THOMAS FLOWERS did sell the land to HENRY McGUFFEY who conveyed to JOHN P. STEGALL whose title has by purchase vested in ISAAC ADAMS. In consideration of the premises and $1.00, said lands are conveyed to ISAAC ADAMS. WILLIAM (X) ALLEN, JR., PRESTON (X) ALLEN, ROBERT (X)BRAGEN, GRACEY (X) BRAGEN, THOMAS (X) KENDRICK. Witness: JOHN AKERS, H. R. HALL, BILL PRICE, JR., JOHN GOODE.

Know all men by these presents that I JOHN A. HAIRSTON of the State of Mississippi, do appoint JESSE CORN my lawful attorney to collect all monies due me in the state of Virginia and North Carolina. I further authorize him to sell all my lands in the State of Virginia with my interest in the Union Iron Works furnace forge land. November 7, 1836. JOHN A. HAIRSTON, BANES CARTER, HENRY YOUNG, J. TURNER.

Deed dated September 15, 1836 between JOSHUA WEST and MARY WEST, his wife, and JEREMIAH WOOD. In consideration of $100.00 conveys 40 acres on Smith River adjoining MARY CONNER. JOSHUA WEST. Witness: NOTLEY P. ADAMS, G. W. CONNER, STEPHEN DEHART.

Deed of trust dated January 1, 1837 between ALVIS LEWIS (Debtor) and BANES CARTER, Trustee, and IRA HURT (creditor). Whereas, Lewis is indebted to Hurt in the sum of $24.34 and desires to secure said debt and does convey the following: 50 acres on Goblintown Creek bounded by WILLIAM VIA and RICHARD MASSEY. ALVIN LEWIS, BANES CARTER, IRA HURT. Witness: WILLIAM PARKER and JOSEPH M. STOVALL.

Deed of trust dated April 29, 1830 between ROBERT AKERS, GEORGE R. DAVIS and WILLIAM AYRES. Whereas, Akers is indebted to Ayres in the sum of $20.00 and being desirous of securing payment of said debt doth grant unto said Davis, Trustee, the following: 1 blind horse (got of JACOB SHELOR); one pided cow and calf (got of THOMAS AUSTIN) with her increase; 9 hogs marked with 2 smooth crops and half crop in the right ear with increase; 1 sheep with increase; 2 feather beds and furniture; 2 pots and hooks; tools and pewter plates. ROBERT (X) AKERS, GEORGE R. DAVIS, WILLIAM AYRES. Witness: JOEL GILBERT, JEFFERSON SNEED.

Commonwealth of Virginia - 1877 - In account with DR. JOHN K. MARTIN June 7 to making post mortem examination of the body of WILLIAM HOWARD THOMAS, making chemical test, and finding arsenious acid in the stomach. $40.00. Sworn to before B. F. SMITH, Justice of the Peace.

Plat of survey for D. S. DEHART 83 acres on Matthews Creek. Dated May 4, 1891. M. E. LEWIS. To P.W. SHELOR, Judge of the County Court: M. E. LEWIS swore to survey of land, DeHart having furnished proof of his having purchased the same at a sale of delinquent lands of the county. May 26, 1891.

Deed dated November 15, 1884 between A. T. MITCHELL and wife and Trustees of DAN RIVER DISTRICT OF PUBLIC SCHOOLS. In consideration of $1.00 doth convey 1/4 of an acre for the purpose of erecting a public school house. A. T. (X) MITCHELL.

Deed dated December 18, 1900 between T. B. BARNARD and M. J. BARNARD, his wife, and J. L. MANKINS' heirs. In consideration of $6.00 conveys a strip of land lying between the lands of J. L. MANKINS' heirs, HAIRSON GOING and COLEMAN GOING, containing 1-1/2 acre, more or less. T. B. BARNARD, J. J. BARNARD. Acknowledged before C.T. McMILLION, Justice of the Peace.

Deed dated March 29, 1877 between JOSEPH HAMMITT of the City of Philadelphia, Pennsylvania, Clergyman, and DEBORAH HAMMITT, his wife, and ANDREW KAMMERER of said city, Real Estate Agent. In consideration of $9,500.00 conveys 1,000 acres excepting a grant of 50 acres. Beginning in the centre of Volunteer Gap Road, being 4-1/2 miles north of state line and parallel to same as shown on a sectional survey by JOSEPH MITCHELL of Fancy Gap adjoining BENJAMIN CHAMBERS' survey. JOSEPH HAMMITT, DEBORAH HAMMITT. Witness: SIMON SNYDER, SAMUEL L. BAYLOR.

Deed dated November 23, 1896, between PETER T. RORRER and NANCY J. RORRER, his wife, of West Virginia; S. G. LAW and SUSAN LAW, his wife; MINTORY FOLEY, all of Virginia; BENJAMIN MEADOWS and GENNARA MEADOWS, his wife, of West Virginia and W. G. RORRER and wife and heirs. In consideration of $194.76 conveys 38 acres known as the Peter Rorrer property. PETER T (X) RORRER, NANCY J. RORRER.

Deed dated August 24, 1828 between GABRIEL DeHART and JESSE P. DeHART. In consideration of $300.00 conveys 150 acres on Joint Crack Creek adjoining GABRIEL DeHART and ELIJAH DeHART. GABRIEL DeHART, E. J. DeHART.

Know all men by these presents that I, JOHN ARNOLD, SR., have this day sold to JOHN ARNOLD, JR. the following property: 1 bay mare supposed to be 11 years old; 1 cow; 2 sows and 10 piggs; 5 shoats and a parsel of corn supposed to be 15 barrels and all my household and kitchen furniture together with all my plantation utensils, fodder and shucks for the purpose of JOHN ARNOLD, JR. is to pay GREENSVILLE PENN $25.00 and also the 600 pounds of tobacco that I was to pay the said Penn for the rent of the land and also $3.50 to WILLIAM KOGER and $7.00 that I am owing JOHN ARNOLD, JR. December 4, 1830. JOHN (X) ARNOLD, SR. Witness: CARRINGTON DILLON, WILLIAM (X) HILL.

Deed of trust dated December 22, 1836 between SHADRACK BEASLEY and WILLIAM CLARK, Trustee, and THOMAS M. CLARK. Whereas, Beasley is indebted to Clark in the sum of $39.41 and he being desirous of securing said debt, doth convey the following: all of his right, title and claim to the estate of his mother, HANNAH BEASLEY. SHADRACK BEASLEY, WILLIAM CLARK. Witness: HENRY DURRAM, ISHAM (X) HOOKER.

Deed dated Mary 7, 1836 between PHILIP VASS and MARTHA VASS. In consideration of 30 lbs. conveys 150 acres on the east side of the mountain on the waters of Johnson's Creek. PHILIP VASS. Witness: PARKER HALL, JEREMIAH McMILLAND, JOHN BOYD.

Deed dated November 25, 1837, between MARTHA VASS and ELIZABETH VASS. Consideration of 30 lbs. conveys 150 acres on east side of the mountain on the headwaters of Johnson Creek. MARTHA VASS. Witness: PHILIP VASS, JOHN VASS.

Articles of Agreement dated September 14, 1833 between USTATIA BUZZARD and PHILIP ASKEW, SR. (leasing). In consideration of $1.00 conveys 3 head of cattle, 2 hogs and all her household and kitchen furniture, and in the further consideration that the said Askew shall support and kindly treat her for and during her natural life, or so long as she may choose to stay with him or his family. ANNESTACIA (X) BUZZARD. Witness: M. SANDEFUR, JOHN GILBERT.

Deed dated _____, 1870, between EWELL BROWN and LUVENIA J. BROWN and JOHN H. TILLEY and CHARLOTT TILLEY, his wife, of Madison County, Kentucky and JOHN F. GRAY. In consideration of $300.00 conveys 233 acres on Russell's Creek. (No signatures)

Received of E. H. HANDY $20.00 in full for a house and lot containing 1 acre, more or less, on the Rye Cove Road at the foot of the Blue Ridge and there being a vendor's lien on the said land, I hereby authorize C. R. MARTIN, Clerk to mark the same satisfied. W. C. RAKES. Acknowledged before T. D. HOWELL, Justice of the Peace.

Deed dated March 21, 1881 between THOMAS T. RAKES and ELIZABETH RAKES, his wife, and DAVID RAKES. In consideration of $90.00 conveys 28-1/2 acres on Ivey Creek. (No signatures)

Deed dated December 21, 1914, between SUSAN A. WEST and J. B. WEST. In consideration of $250.00 conveys her entire dower rights and any other rights that she has in the old home tract of land on Dan River, it being the same land the heirs of W. J. WEST, deceased, deed to J. B. WEST and E. P. WEST. SUSAN A. WEST.

Bill of Sale dated January 9, 1917, between W. C. CRADDOCK and

J. H. TILLEY. In consideration of $26.25 conveys 1 yoke of steers, one red and the other white spotted, and known as the "MOSE HARRIS" CATTLE. W.C. CRADDOCK. Acknowledged before J. S. TAYLOR, Clerk.

Deed dated February 10, 1888, between I. N. AKERS and NANCY V. AKERS, his wife, and JAMES A. HUGHES. In consideration of $225.00 conveys a tract of land on the waters of South Mayo. I.N. AKERS, N.V. AKERS. Acknowledged before WILLIAM W. MOIR, Commissioner in Chancery and T. D. HOWELL, Justice of the Peace.

Know all men by these presents that we D.C. GALLANT and MARSHALL WILLIAMS are firmly bound unto the Commonwealth of Virginia in the sum of $200.00. The condition of the above obligation is that the said D.C. GALLANT has this day contracted with the County Court of Patrick for the maintenance and care of RUTH J. GALLANT, a lunatic, now confined in jail under the decision of 3 justices until she may be further dealt with as the law directs. April 25, 1876. D.C. (X) GALLANT, MARSHALL (X) WILLIAMS.

Agreement dated October 17, 1881 between FANNIE NOWLIN and M. M. GILBERT. Whereas Nowlin has rented to Gilbert a certain house and garden at the foot of the hill below her tavern property for the ensuing year for the sum of $25.00, which sum is to be expended in improving the said property. The said Gilbert is to have the house and garden and 1 apple tree in the back yard and as much manure as is necessary for said garden. Possession to be given on November 1, 1881. F. NOWLIN, M. M. GILBERT.

Deed dated September 18, 1842, between WILLIAM EAST and POLLY CANNON. In consideration of $1,000.00 conveys 490 acres composed of 2 tracts adjoining ISHAM EAST. WILLIAM EAST. Witness: THOMAS C. GREENWOOD, JOHN HICKS, ISHAM EAST.

(Top part missing) proved November 1796. Deed between FRANCIS GRIMES and GEORGE HAIRSTON of Henry County. Description of lands missing, but mentions Merruage Plantation. FRANCIS GRAHAM(?) Witness: SAMUEL HINSON, CHARLES CRUMP, JAMES HORD, WILLIAM HORD.

Deed dated April 12, 1912, between R. H. FAIN and LUMMIE FAIN and W. A. CASSELL. In consideration of $150.00 conveys 14-1/2 acres in Dan River District. R. H. FAIN, LUMLEY FAIN. (Signatures not notarized)

Deed dated December 6, 1890 between BEVERLY L. GUNTER and E. F. GUNTER, his wife, and R. M. PEATROSS. Conveys a tract of land on the waters of Peters Creek and being a portion of the land formerly belonging to JOHN JOYCE and known as Lot No. 3 alloted to NANCY JONES and being the same land PETER D. JONES and NANCY JONES, his wife, by deed dated June 19, 1890 and recorded in Deed Book 25, conveyed to indemnify F. P. HALL (by reason of his signing as security a bond to J. J. COLLINS for $200.00). B. S. GUNTER, E. F. GUNTER. Acknowledged before WILLIAM WITT, Justice of the Peace.

Deed dated September 25, 1804 between FEATHERSTONE WALDEN and

JACOB BLACKBURN. In consideration of 30 lbs. conveys 50 acres on Goblintown Creek adjoining JOHN INGRUM, ISHAM CRADDOCK and MOSES WALDEN. FEATHERSTONE WALDEN. Witness: MOSES WALDEN, BENJAMIN MIZE, DAVID MIZE.

Deed dated April 25, 1808 between PAUL HOWELL and PHILISTON HOWELL, SAMUEL HOWELL and JAMES HOWELL, my three youngest sons. In consideration of $1.00 and love and affection, conveys to Philiston my plantation known as the red cabin meeting house, and to Samuel from that line down to the crossroads that runs on the ridge that divides the big branch from the river, and to James my plantation on Dan River where I now live. My sons are not entitled to the profits from the lands until after the death of my wife Patsy and myself and after that they may dispose of the lands as they please. PAUL HOWELL. Witness: JNO HUGHES, GAB. PENN and WILLIAM CARTER.

Deed dated March 5, 1847 between AUSTIN PROPHET and WILLIAM LEE of Floyd County. In consideration of $80.00 conveys 125 acres on Poppler Camp Creek lying mostly in Patrick County, adjoining CHARLES THOMAS CONNER.   AUSTIN (X) PROPHET.   Witness: JEREMIAH BURNETT, JAMES BRAMMER, CHRISTOPHER LAYMON, JOHN SHORTT.

Deed dated May 10, 1839 between JOHN MARTIN of Surry County, North Carolina and THOMAS MARTIN of same. In consideration of $400.00 conveys 200 acres in Patrick on both sides of Johnson's Creek. JOHN MARTIN. Witness: JAMES (X) HALEY.

April Term, 1875 - C. M. STIGGLER, Plaintiff v. NATHANIEL FISHER, deceased, Admr. To: WILLIAM M. TREDWAY, Judge of the Circuit Court: Report of the estate of NATHANIEL FISHER, deceased. ISAAC N. AKERS, Admr. has filed his inventory stating no personal effect has come into his hands. Commissioner finds 300 acres on the south fork of Rock Castle Creek less an off-conveyance of 20 acres in the name of NATHANIEL FISHER.

JAMES A. DeHART - 1888, 1889, and 1890 - 6-1/2 acres, value $39.00. State tax 12 cents; school tax 4 cents; county tax 1 cent; district school tax 2 cents; R R tax 39 cents; county levy 13 cents. Total 71 cents. T. C. ADAMS, Treasurer.

Agreement dated April 5, 1905 between PETER JOHNSON and JOYCE & SHELTON. In consideration of $65.00 conveys one black mare about 12 years old. PETER (X) JOHNSON.

Deed dated June 7, 1877 between SAMUEL G. STAPLES and CAROLINE STAPLES, his wife, and JERRY STAPLES, JAMES STAPLES, BENJAMIN HAIRSTON, PRESTON HUGHES and JAMES GOING, Trustees for the AFRICAN METHODIST EPISCOPAL CHURCH. In consideration of the desire for Christian religion among the colored people of Patrick County, hereby conveys to Trustees one lot of land situated on the Wytheville and Danville Turnpike just below the residence of W. J. NOEL, adjoining COLO. JNO E. PENN to be used as a place of religious worship or school and for no other purpose. SAMUEL G. STAPLES, C. H. STAPLES.

Deed dated September 9, 1879 between ABRAM ROBERSON and A. W. HOUCHINS. To secure payment of a bond for $169.07 to ALFRED ELGIN, conveys 127 acres on Joint Crack Creek bounded by LANDON ROBERSON, JAMES R. TURNER, JOHN W. DeHART, it being the land on which Roberson now resides. ABRAM ROBERSON. Acknowledged before JOHN A. BURNETT, Justice of the Peace.

Deed dated February 25, 1901 between E. G. NEWMAN and JETTIE NEWMAN, his wife, and J. F. EDWARDS. In consideration of $8.75 conveys 1/24 acres on the waters of Ivy Creek adjoining G. L. THOMAS. E. G. NEWMAN. Acknowledge before T. A. HUNT, Deputy Clerk.

Deed of trust dated April 23, 1846 between ELIJAH DeHART and JAMES VIA and CHARLES DeHART. Whereas Elijah DeHart is indebted to Charles DeHart in the sum of $40.00 and in order to secure said debt coneys 1 chestnut sorrel mare; 4 cattle; 3 sheep; 25 hogs with increase; and household and kitchen furniture. ELIJAH DeHART, JAMES VIA, CHARLES DeHART. Witness: W. C. ROBERTSON, WILLIAM DeHART.

Last Will and Testament of WILLIAM BRISTOW dated July 31, 1792. Bequeaths whole state to wife, MARGARET BRISTOW, during her life unless she marries and if she marries, everything to be divided equally among my beloved children (not named). BENJAMIN BRISTOW, JR., JAMES INGRUM and JAMES COX, Executors. WILLIAM BRISTOW. Witness: JAMES COX, JAMES (X) INGRUM, SARAH A (X) BISHOP.

We the undersigned legatees under the will of ELIJAH DeHART, deceased, do hereby authorize and empower CHARLES DeHART, Executor, to sell all of the estate, both real and personal, left by the Last Will and Testament of MARY DeHART, Widow of Elijah, and payment to be applied to those entitled under the will. December 13, 1847. THOMAS DeHART, WILSON T. VAUGHAN, R. C. THOMAS, JAMES VIA, D. P. TAYLOR, AARON DeHART, Z. T. DeHART, FOUNTAIN HOWELL.

Last Will and Testament of JAMES NOWLIN dated March 31, 1803. I desire that my wife, USLEY NOWLIN, may keep all of my estate in her hands until her decease unless the children now living single should marry before her death and if they do, she may give to each of them as much as the ones now married have received. FRANCIS NOWLIN and CLABOURN SHELTON Co-Executors. JAMES (X) NOWLIN. Witness: I. DODSON, JOHN HANBY, JR., ROBERT SHARP. Memorandum: Prior to my Last Will and Testament I agreed to lend out of my stock of cattle to my son, Francis, 2 steers and 1 heifer which he is to replace to the estate when wanting.

H. W. REYNOLDS in his lifetime sold to ABRAM REYNOLDS (colored) 100 acres at $5.00 per acre and he has been paid for it, the land not yet being accurately located. It is bounded as near as can be ascertained as follows: commencing at the road by the Critz and Lee's store where his outside line comes to the road, thence back to the cross fence and then with the cross fence in the direction of the Homestead to the branch; thence with the branch to the road by the Lee Store where he lives to the Homestead; thence with the road towards the Homestead to a poplar tree on the north side of the road, thence towards the mountain, then back southward to the Lee line, then down the Lee line far enough to leave the old well at the house on the hill, northwest of the line to the road and with the road to the beginning.

We the adult heirs of said Reynolds and to secure to ABRAM REYNOLDS a good and lawful title as the heirs become of age and hereby confirm all our interest in the same. A. M. LYBROOK, A. D. REYNOLDS, P. J. REYNOLDS, H. H. REYNOLDS, W. R. REYNOLDS, W. N. REYNOLDS, N.K. REYNOLDS, ROBERT CRITZ, N. J. REYNOLDS, LUCIE B. CRITZ, MARY J. LYBROOK - June 2, 1881.

Know all men by these presents that I, LUCINDA A. BARKER of the State of Louisiana but now sojourning in Surry County, North Carolina and Patrick County, Virginia, do appoint THOMAS BOYLES of Surry County, North Carolina, my attorney to sell all the lands I hold or may hereafter have a right to in the County of Patrick, as one of the heirs of WILLIAM BOYLES, deceased, of Stokes County, North Carolina. May 14, 1848. LUCINDA A. (X) BARKER. Witness: ELISHA COLLINGS, A. T. COLLINGS.

Know all men by these presents that I, EZEKIEL MORRIS, being about to leave this county and state do appoint JOSEPH REYNOLDS as my attorney to act in my behalf against the claims of JAMES ELKINS and JONATHAN ISOM in a tract of land on the north side of Rock Castle Creek, contents and boundaries as by copy grant, and in my behalf to bring suit for the defence of the said tract, Elkins having sold the land to Isom and Isom to me, and also 6 acres which I bought from Isom adjoining this tract. November 5, 1802. EZEKIEL MORRIS. Witness: GEORGE (X) BRAMMER, SAMUEL HARRIS, WILLIAM (X) SLON.

Know all men by these presents that I, SAMUEL CLARKE, WILLIAM FRANS, THOMAS J. TATUM, CARDWELL CLARK, THOMAS P. CLARK, EMMERREE R. CLARK, DAVID M. CLARK and JEREMIAH HYLTON, heirs of GEORGE CLARK, deceased, and SARAH CLARK, widow and relict of GEORGE CLARK, deceased, do hereby appoint DAVID BURGE of Jackson County, Missouri, our attorney to collect all monies due us in the State of Virginia as heirs of said estate. August 3, 1842. SAMUEL CLARK, WILLIAM FRANS, THOMAS J. TATUM, CARDWELL CLARK, THOMAS P. CLARK, EMMERREE R. CLARK, DAVID M. CLARK, JEREMIAH HYLTON, and SARAH (X) CLARK. (All signatures notarized in Jackson County, Missouri, FRANKLIN SMITH, Justice of the Peace.)

Deed dated October 20, 1837 between ALEXANDER JOYCE and ANDREW JOYCE. In consideration of $502.00 conveys 250 acres on Elk Creek adjoining JOHN JOYCE. ALEXANDER JOYCE, LUCY R. (X) JOYCE.

Deed dated November 3, 1825 between GOLEHUGH MOORE of Surry County, North Carolina and EDMON BINGHAM of Halifax County, Virginia. In consideration of $300.00 conveys 102 acres on both sides of Johnson's Creek. GOLEHUE MOORE. Witness: SAMUEL

FORKNER, WILLIAM CROWDER, JACOB GRIGG, OWEN EAST.

Office of the Treasurer of Patrick County - Real estate sold in the month of January, 1889, for non-payment of taxes - J. A. DeHART 6-1/2 acres on Widgeon Creek, Purchaser C. C. HOUCHINS. Purchase price - $1.19. ISAAC C. ADAMS.

Deed dated April 12, 1827 between JAMES HARRIS and KIZZIAH HARRIS, his wife, and MARTIN DILLION. In consideration of 1,000 pounds of tobacco conveys 31 acres on Mayo River bounded by THOMAS PENN, WILLIAM ELLIOTT and JESSE REYNOLDS. JAMES HARRIS, KEZZIAH HARRIS. Witness: DAVID R. PEDIGO, JOSEPH COX, JAMES BOYD.

Deed dated September __, 1811 between WILLIAM WITT and WILLIAM KEATON. In consideration of 60 pounds conveys 180 acres in the Flat Hollow. WILLIAM WITT, LUCY (X) WITT. Witness: EDWARD PHILPOTT, JOSIAH RIEVES, THOMAS SNEED, GABRIEL PENN.

Deed dated December 8, 1800 between JAMES HOLLANDSWORTH and SIMON DOTSON. In consideration of $50.00 conveys 25 acres on Wites Branch, a fork of Blackberry Creek. JAMES (X) HOLLANDSWORTH, REBECAK (X) HOLLANDSWORTH. Witness: JAMES BAKER, DAVID BAKER, WILLIAM (X) DOTSON .

June 2, 1848, I do hereby transfer to MARTIN CLOUD the benefit of an order made by the County Court some courts since directing the Overseers of the Poor to bind JOSEPHUS GOING, son of HANNAH GOING, to me as I do not intend to have said boy bound to me. JAMES NOWLIN. Witness: PURVIS AYRES.

Deed dated March 4, 1833 between JAMES DUVALL and ABSLAM SHELTON. In consideration of $50.00 conveys 50 acres by survey adjoining JAMES NUMAN on the waters of Russell Creek. ABSLOM SHELTON, MARY (X) SHELTON. Witness: JAMES C. SOUTHERN, M. T. CLARKE.

Agreement between L.B. WEST and JAMES RANGELEY. West agrees to sell to Rangeley a piece of land, being the south end of his tract and bounded on the north by S. G. Staples and WILLIAM L. McCANLESS and including the land which Rangeley is now clearing for the sum of $6.00 per acre. (Not dated) L. B. WEST

Deed of trust dated January 25, 1858 between TIRA PACK and ANDREW LYBROOK. Pack grants to Lybrook the following property: 2 head of cattle with 1 cow and yearlin marked with a cross slit, swallow fork in the right ear, and all household and kitchen furniture to secure a debt of $4.00 to SAMUEL G. STAPLES. TIRA (X) PACK.

Deed dated December 23, 1823 between JACOB PRILEAMAN and others appointed Commissioners by the Court in the case of ADRON NOE, Plaintiff and ROBIN FRAZIER and others, Defendants, conveyed to AARON NOE 150 acres on the south side of Smith River. LEWIS FOSTER, CHARLES (X) SMITH, JACOB PRILLAMAN. Witness: HAMPTON

HAYNES, JOHN (X) BELL, WILEY D. WOODS.

Deed dated October 13, 1795 between SAMUEL SHELTON and JAMES ENNIS. In consideration of 50 pounds conveys 78 acres on the south side of North Mayo River. SAMUEL SHELTON. Witness: JOHN MILLER, JOSEPH TAYLOR.

Know all men by these presents that I, DOCIA R. PEDIGO, MARY E. PEDIGO and MALISSE D. PEDIGO, hereby appoint WILLIAM B. PEDIGO to sign our names as security on the bond of CHARLES L. PEDIGO as Administrator of ELIJAH PEDIGO, deceased, and on the bond of A.L. PEDIGO as committee for BETTIE PEDIGO. February 2, 1892. DOCIA R. PEDIGO, MARY E. PEDIGO, MALISSE D. PEDIGO. Acknowledged before H. H. HALL, a Justice of the Peace.

Deed dated March 6, 1880 between PATSY ROGERS and POLLY ROGERS and SALLIE ROGERS. In consideration of the love and affection and the sum of $1.00, their kindness to me in the past and their care and maintenance of me in the future, conveys all of her personal estate. PATSY (X) ROGERS. Witness: LUCINDA P. SHELTON, T. F. SHELTON. Acknowledged before L. G. RUCKER, Clerk.

Agreement dated September __, 1902, between F. D. LAWLESS and G. W. LAWLESS. In consideration of the love and affection F.D. LAWLESS has for her father-in-law, she conveys the right to live on and cultivate rent free 50 acres on the waters of Mill Creek which was this date conveyed to me by the heirs of ROSANA M. LAWLESS, deceased. F. D. LAWLESS. Acknowledged before R. E. WOOLWINE, Deputy Clerk.

Know all men by these presents that I, WILLIAM WISLER, ALBERT H. SMITH and JESSE E. SMITH do appoint JESSE W. SMITH our attorney to execute and acknowledge a bond before the Clerk of Court in the penalty of $2,000.00 for the grant of administration of the estate of JOSEPH S. SMITH, deceased, to C. C. SMITH. July 1, 1882. WILLIAM WISLER, ALBERT H. SMITH, JESSE E. SMITH.

Deed dated September 5, 1844 between WILLIAM McMILLIAN, SR. and HENRY YOUNG. In consideration of $35.56 conveys 82 acres on both sides of Sons Run, this being the land purchased of Dillard and Bellar adjoining NATHANIEL YOUNG, JOHN BOWMAN, CLARENCE BOWMAN, GEORGE SMITH and ARON BOWMAN. WILLIAM (X) McMILLAND. Witness: A. BOWMAN, CLEM BOWMAN, R. N. LOWE, THOMAS CLARK.

Look for deed JOHN C. MARTIN to THOMAS S. ADAMS for 125 acres transferred in 1873. The deed was handed in the office May 1, 1871 and paid for as per receipt.

A matter of dispute having arisen between T. D. RORRER and CHARLES H. BOWMAN, as to whether the said Rorrer has a right of lien upon a horse claimed by Bowman and claimed exempt under the poor law, the parties have agreed that the matter be submitted to WILLIAM WITT and MURRY TURNER and A. J. STEADMAN, the umpire selected by the said arbitrators. February 5, 1878. T.D. (X)

RORRER, C.H. (X) BROWN. Teste: WILLIAM W. MOIR.
We the arbitrators are of the opinion that CHARLES H. BOWMAN is not a housekeeper in the meaning of the law and therefore is not entitled to the horse under the exemption law but is liable to sale under the trust deed.

Deed dated June 13, 1885 between SAMUEL G. STAPLES and CAROLINE H. STAPLES, his wife, and SALLIE HUNT STAPLES, wife of ABRAM P. STAPLES. That for a valuable consideration heretofore paid conveys a lot in the Town of Stuart on the northwest side of the Wytheville and Danville Turnpike adjoining a lot now owned by ABRAM F. MAY, 40 x 100 feet square, fronting 40 feet on the turnpike and running back 100 feet. SAMUEL G. STAPLES, C. H. STAPLES. Acknowledged before SAMUEL H. HOGE.

Whereas, SAMUEL H. HOGE has been appointed Commissioner to sell real estate and collect the purchase money for the Circuit Court of Patrick County in cases therein pending. Know all men by these presents that I, JOHN E. PENN, appoint the said Hoge as my attorney to execute as surety for said Hoge any bond in my name which he may be required to give as such Commissioner. JOHN E. PENN, November 11, 1884. Acknowledged in Roanoke County.

Deed dated March 23, 1818 between JOHN BARRETT and ELIZABETH BARRETT, his wife, and ABRAM STAPLES. In consideration of $150.00 conveys 369 acres by survey on the waters of South Mayo River, it being 1/2 of the land FRANCIS BARRETT, deceased, died seized of and which fell to JOHN BARRETT, and being his 1/4 part of the 369 acres which descended to the said JOHN BARRETT, ELIZABETH BARRETT and SARAH BARRETT the 3 children of FRANCIS and his widow, SUSANNAH FAIN, adjoining ELIPHAZ SHELTON, SAMUEL STAPLES, and the widow Hanby's place. JOHN (X) BARRETT, ELIZABETH (X) BARRETT. Witness: GEORGE LAYMAN, PETER (X) CASSELL, ELIZABETH HARRIS.

Deed dated April 1, 1835 between A. STAPLES, Clerk of the County Court, and ABRAM STAPLES and JAMES M. REDD. Whereas under the act for the sale of lands for non-payment of taxes, the land mentioned herein was assessed in the name of NATHANIEL ANDERSON and by assessment $1.00 was assessed for the year 1832. Whereas, said Anderson was not in occupancy of the land nor was it occupied by any other person, and whereas, taxes were not paid to the Sheriff. In consequence JAMES W. WAUHOP, Deputy for EDWARD PHILPOTT, Sheriff, did advertise the lands for sale as proper to do and at the sale GILBERT BOWMAN became the purchaser of 5,000 acres of land aforesaid and by deed dated November 29, 1834, the said Bowman transferred to Staples and Redd all his title in the lands. In consideration of $2.00 taxes due, damages and costs, conveys 5,000 acres on Dan River adjoining WILLIAM McLEN & CO., JOHN D. CHEATHAM, JOHN MILLER. A. STAPLES, Clerk (This deed is bound together in book form with thread.)

To: P. W. SHEYLOR, Judge of the County Court. The undersigned make the following report. By virtue of a deed of trust executed to the undersigned by WILLIAM J. JEFFERSON and

LOUCINDA E. JEFFERSON to secure ALEXANDER RAKES certain debts and the Grantors having defaulted in payment, after having been advertised as the law requires, said land was sold to GEORGE W. VIA and E. T. M. VIA for $318.00, and the aforesaid lands are conveyed for the consideration of $299.25. A. P. ROBERTSON, Trustee.

Know all men by these presents that we GABRIEL HYLTON and CAMILLUS KING are bound unto VALENTINE HYLTON and GEORGE W. HYLTON in the sum of $2,500.00. Dated November 8, 1850. The condition of this obligation is such that VALENTINE HYLTON and GEORGE W. HYLTON have qualified as Executors of JEREMIAH W. HYLTON, deceased, and have sold a portion of the property and the estate now being in a condition to distribute among the heirs and distributees, and the Executors having advanced to GABRIEL HYLTON $2,500.00, his portion under the will of Jeremiah, and the said GABRIEL HYLTON and his security now bind themselves to indemnify said Executors from any damage they may sustain in any way from the said advancement. GABRIEL HYLTON, CAMILLUS KING. Witness: GEORGE PANNILL.

There is included in this file a like document from CAMILLUS KING and GABRIEL HYLTON, his security, FOR THE ADVANCEMENT OF $2,500.00 to CAMILLUS KING as his share under the will of JEREMIAH HYLTON.

Also a like document from GEORGE W. CLANTON and GEORGE OVERSTREET, his security, for an advancement to Clanton for the same.

A like document from GEORGE OVERSTREET the lawful attorney and guardian of the heirs of JEREMIAH HYLTON, deceased, an advancement for the same amount.

Same document from GABRIEL HYLTON, Guardian for AUSTIN HYLTON, and CAMILLUS KING, his security, for the advancement of $2,500.00 to Gabriel as the share due Austin.

Same document from CAMILLUS KING, Guardian for NANCY JANE HYLTON, and GABRIEL HYLTON, his security, for the advancement of $2,500.00 to King as the share due Nancy Jane.

Same document from GEORGE OVERSTREET and CAMILLUS KING, his security, for advancement to Overstreet of $2,500.00, his share under the will.

(All documents dated November 8, 1850, and all witnessed by GEORGE PANNILL.)

Deed dated July 23, 1866, between BRAXTON PURDY and JOHN W. PURDY. Consideration of $100.00 conveys 75 acres on North Mayo, adjoining JAMES HARRIS. BRAXTON PURDY.

Deed dated October 17, 1831, between CLABOURNE SHELTON and ELIZABETH SHELTON, his wife, and JAMES M. REED. Consideration of $600.00 conveys 3 tracts of land, first containing 190 acres by survey on the waters of South Mayo River; second bounded by

22

aforesaid tract, HUDSON SHELTON, SAMUEL HOWEL, it being the same purchased from ABRAM STAPLES and JAMES M. REDD and by them from ELIPHAZ SHELTON'S estate, the metes and bounds to be ascertained from a grant in the possession of Redd; third containing 50 acres devised to CLABOURNE SHELTON by his deceased father, ELIPHAZ SHELTON, and known as the Coss tract. (No signatures)

Articles of Agreement dated September 17, 1859, between SAMUEL G. STAPLES and JAMES W. FRASURE. Staples has leased to Frasure for the term of 5 years, 75 acres on the north side of Danville and Withville Turnpik adjoining LEVI SPENCER and WILLIAM N. WEST, with the right to underlet the same to any respectable man and the use of the timber for sale or otherwise, and the said Frashure agrees on his part to build a good and comfortable log house on the premises, corn crib, smoke house, stables and other necessary buildings and a large tobacco barn, and to enclose the orchard and prune the trees. SAMUEL G. STAPLES, JAMES W. FRASHURE. Teste: H. TUGGLE.
I assign the above to WILLOUGHBY BLACKARD for value received October 24, 1835. JAMES W. FRASHURE.

Deed dated November 1, 1855, between MARY J. PINKARD of the County of Albermarle and HORACE M. PINKARD of the County of Franklin. In consideration of the love and affection for her son doth loan unto the said HORACE PINKARD a bay horse, with saddle and bridle, said property to be returned to her or her estate when called for. MARY J. PINKARD, HORACE M. PINKARD. Acknowledged before DANIEL PERROW, a Justice of the Peace for Albermarle County.

Deed dated April 25, 1881, between SPENCER F. NOWLIN and GEORGE W. GILBERT, SAM T. GILBERT and R. D. YEATTS. In consideration of $5.00 conveys 1/2 acre on the road leading from the Courthouse towards Winston-Salem on the south side of said road, for the use of a public school forever. S. F. NOWLIN.

Deed dated June 17, 1870, between WILLIAM A. BALDWIN and MARY L. BALDWIN, his wife, of Camden County, New Jersey and JOSEPH HAMMITT, Minister of the gospel of Point Pleasant, Pennsylvania. In consideration of $6,000.00 conveys 1500 acres and being a part of the BENJAMIN CHAMBERS survey in Carroll and Patrick Counties and conveyed said Chambers by the Commonwealth of Virginia January, 1776, and part of a survey by JAMES S. MITCHELL in 1863. Acknowledged in Camden County, NJ before SAMUEL WILLS. (Signatures missing from document.)

Deed dated May 7, 1887, between E. W. BARKSDALE and F. G. RUFFIN, JR. Consideration of $350.00 conveys all of his interest in walnut lumber and timber that he now owns in Patrick County, and tools used in getting said walnut. E. W. BARKSDALE.

Deed dated August 27, 1886 between ELIZABETH A. FITZGERALD and ELAM P. NEWMAN. In consideration of $51.00 conveys her interest in the land of which ELAM NEWMAN died seized and possessed on the waters of South Mayo adjoining S. F. NOWLIN and THOMAS SHELTON.

ELIZABETH A. FITZGERALD. Teste: L. G. RUCKER, Clerk.

Know all men by these presents that I SARAH PORTIS do appoint LEWIS INSCORE my attorney to collect anything due me by MILTON MONTGOMERY or other persons. March 23, 1878. SARAH (X) PORTIS. Acknowledged before L. D. McMILLION, Justice of the peace.

Agreement between E. L. CLARK, GEORGE T. MONFORD and SAM LYBROOK and J. P. GILBERT of Thomasville, North Carolina. In consideration of $4,000.00 due October 12, 1906 convey property known as Stuart Manufacturing Co. containing 1-5\8 acres and all buildings and machines thereon. J. P. GILBERT. In case sale made we will pay 10% commission.

Deed dated January 7, 1886, between W. T. AKERS, Trustee in a deed of trust executed by KELLY MONTGOMERY on November 13, 1872 and M. TURNER, he being the highest bidder at the sale of said lands. In consideration of $50.00 conveys 50 acres on the waters of Johnson's Creek adjoining ROBERT MARSHALL. W. T. AKERS.

(Top part missing) Deed between L.G. RUCKER, Clerk, and D. S. DeHART. Conveys 83 acres on the waters of Mathews Creek adjoining A. W. WIMBISH and FRANCIS TUGGLE. (No signatures)

Know all men by these presents that I, JOHN BRYANT, SR., have this day given to JOHN MARTIN and ANNIE MARTIN, the children of LUISA MARTIN, to be equally divided between them 1 side board now at GREEN WRIGHT'S; 1 cupboard at BETTY BRYANT'S; 1 burrow now at BETTY BRYANT'S; 2 beadsteads now at BETTY BRYANT'S; 1 bed and 2 candle stands now at BETTY BRYANT'S; 1 milk cow and all other property not mentioned. I reserve the control of said property as long as I live but at my death said property with all other property of every kind including 1 bond I now hold against my 2 daughters, BETTY BRYANT and NANCY FOLEY, for $25.00 if not collected during my lifetime, shall transfer in consideration of the love and affection I have for them and in the further consideration of their kind attention and waiting on me in my old age in the past and the desire that they continue to do so. September 16, 1895. JOHN (X) BRYANT. Acknowledged before C. R. MARTIN, Clerk.

Deed dated December 25, 1874 between SAMUEL G. STAPLES, attorney in fact for CYRUS P. MENDENHALL and NANCY S. MENDENHALL, his wife, formerly NANCY S. STAPLES, and JOSEPH COLLINS. By Power of Attorney dated May 1, 1874, Mendenhalls appointed Staples as their attorney in fact to sell all lands devised to NANCY MENDENHALL under the will of ABRAM STAPLES, deceased, to S. G. STAPLES and W. N. STAPLES, Trustees for the said NANCY STAPLES. In consideration of $35.00 conveys 30 acres on Elk Creek, part of the tract known as the Martindale land and adjoining JOHN S. STANLEY, THOMAS M. CLARK, SEATON COLLINS, WILLIAM BURGE, JACK COLLINS and JOSEPH COLLINS. SAMUEL G. STAPLES, Attorney in Fact.

Deed dated February 5, 1825, between WILLIAMSON SMITH of Murry

County, Tennessee, and WILLIAM CARTER. Consideration of $75.00 conveys 50 acres on Bell's Spur, part of Bell's order. WILLIAMSON SMITH. Witness: WILLIAM CARTER, JR., SUSAN D. CARTER, ELIZABETH CARTER.

Inventory and appraisement of the estate of WILLIAM CARTER, deceased, includes various items of personal property and household furniture, farm animal, including oxen and 2 mules, 1 bay horse DON QUIXOTE, 1 bay horse RODOLPHUS, 1 bay horse MARK ANTHONY, 1 bay horse STUMBLE, 1 colt, 2 old stills and copper worms; 1 old black man ABRAM - $200; 1 old black woman PHILIS - $00; 1 old black woman MILLY - $00; 1 old black man - $00; 1 old black woman JUNE - $25; 1 negro AUSTIN - $500; 1 negro PETER - $400; 1 negro LEWIS - $450; 1 black woman AMERICA and child - $400; 1 boy HENRY - $400; 1 boy ARON - $300; 1 black boy OSCAR - $200; 1 black girl EMILY - $500; 1 black woman MARTHA - $400; 1 black woman CATHERINE - $300; 1 black woman LUCY $250; (No total value listed). JOSEPH SMITH, ISHAM BARNET, D. B. HATCHER, December Court, 1846. SAMUEL STAPLES, Deputy Clerk.

Bonds and accounts in the possession of WILLIAM CARTER. GILBERT BOWMAN total $250 (according to a verbal understanding between Carter and Bowman, a suit in process to sell the lands. However, Bowman still in possession); GORDON McCRAW $85.00; WILLIAM BLANCET $6; JOHN KING $100; DANIEL EPPERSON $154; JOHN BOYD $50; DAVID GRAHAM $110; TIRA BARNARD $1.22 (barred and uncollected); C. HARRIS $.18 (insolvent); ARON BOWMAN $12.25 (insolvent and out of date); H. H. MOORE $22.26 (insolvent); WILLIAM SMITH $1.68 (deceased insolvent); MARTIN DUNCAN $21.52 (insolvent); G. L. BREAM $.30 (denied and uncollected); GILBERT BOWMAN $2.63 (insolvent); JOHN COLLINS $4.15 (out of date and uncollected); CLEMENT R. VAUGHAN $.94 (denied and uncollected); GEORGE BOWMAN $.80 (out of date, denied and uncollected); HAMON BOWMAN $3.61 (out of date and insolvent); JAMES SMITH $2 (out of date and uncollected); JESSE THOMPSON $5 (insolvent); SHADRACK BEASLEY $5 (out of date and uncollected); ELIJAH DICKERSON $5.81 (out of date and uncollected); JOHN HICKS $4.78 (insolvent); WILLIAM DURHAM $.50 (insolvent); ARCHABAL BOWMAN $.70 (out of date and uncollected); JUDITH HENSLEY $2.66 (out of date and insolvent); GEORGE W. KING $20.99 (out of date and uncollected); JOSIAH MOREFILED (removed) $7.87; JAMES WATKINS (removed) $2.25; SAMUEL HUGHES $11.58 (out of date and uncollected); WALKER CARTER $1.69 (denied could not prove it). HAMON CRITZ $11.67 (out of date and uncollected); NELSON THOMPSON $.16 (out of date and uncollected; THOMAS SCOTT $.32 (out of date and uncollected); E. M. BOWMAN $.37-/2 (the debtor not found, supposed to be worthless). A. H. CARTER, M.D. CARTER, Executors of WILLIAM CARTER, deceased. (This document is sewn together with thread in book form.)

Deed dated July 2, 1870 between SAMUEL G. STAPLES and CAROLINE STAPLES, his wife, and CHARLES M. SHELTON (son of THOMAS SHELTON). In consideration of $400.00 conveys 46 acres by survey on South Mayo River. SAMUEL G. STAPLES.

Deed of Gift dated January 3, 1883 between WILLIAM P. FLOYD

and JANE FLOYD. In consideration of the love and affection I have for my daughter and divers other good causes, conveys 1 cow and yearling, all household and kitchen furniture. WILLIAM P. FLOYD. Witness: JOHN A. FLOYD, J. H. MORISON.

Deed dated June 28, 1881 between A. J. STEDMAN, Special Commissioner and JAMES W. THOMAS. Whereas Stedman was appointed Special Commissioner in the cause of ABRAM ROBERSON and wife against RUTH HATCHER and others. In consideration of $130.00 conveys a tract of land that belonged to the estate of BURWELL HATCHER, deceased, on the waters of Widgeon Creek, containing 100 acres, subject to the right of dower of his widow. A. J. STEDMAN, Special Commissioner.

Deed dated April 16, 1887 between JNO HURD, P.H. LYBROOK and A. D. REYNOLDS. Whereas P. H. LYBROOK and JNO HURD are now the joint owners of the soapstone mineral deposit purchased by JNO HURD from ISAAC JONES on a tract of land on Ingram's Creek, being the land Jones purchased from W. C. LEMONS, together with rights of ingress and egress, for the development of the soapstone quarries. In consideration of $75.00 conveys 1/3 interest to A.D. REYNOLDS. JOHN HURD, P.H. LYBROOK, A.D. REYNOLDS.

Office of the Treasurer - List of real estate sold January, 1888 for non-payment of taxes - 108 acres in the name of J. H. MARTIN and D. S. DeHART. Purchase money $3.46 (amount of taxes). Purchaser, D. S. DeHART. I.C. ADAMS, Treasurer.

Deed dated May 14, 1831 between WILLIAM ARNOLD and GREENSVILLE PENN and PETER P. PENN & CO. That Arnold is indebted to GREENSVILLE PENN fore $11.00. In consideration of $1.00 Arnold conveys to P. P PENN 1 brown colored no horns cow and 2 dark colored yearlings; 1 yoke of oxen, one black and the other red, about 3 years old, to secure payment of the aforesaid debt. WILLIAM ARNOLD, GREENSVILLE PENN, PETER P. PENN & CO. Witness: JOHN CHERRY.

County Court - May 7, 1891 - D. S. DeHART presented a plat of a tract of land and certificate of survey for the land on Matthews Creek sold for non-payment of taxes on February 28, 1888, and purchased by him. It is ordered that the Clerk record same and execute a deed to him. WILLIAM W. MOIR, Deputy Clerk.

Deed dated November 4, 1794 between JOSEPH BOYD and DAVID McGOWN. Consideration of 100 pounds conveys 114 acres on the north fork of Johnson's Creek. JOSEPH BOYD, JOHN BOYD. Witness: MUMFORD SMITH, SAMUEL CANNON, MOSSES REA.

Whereas, JOHN TATUM hath sued out of County Court a writ of capias against the bodies of CHRISTOPHER BINGHAM and RICHARD PICKEREL for a debt of $45.75. Whereas, A.B. CLARK Deputy for CHARLES FOSTER, Sheriff, did arrest Bingham and confine him in the jail, and whereas the said Bingham having rendered a schedule of his whole estate consisting in part of an interest in 260 acres in

Pittsylvania County, and took the oath of an insolvent debtor. Now therefore this indenture dated July 20, 1836 between CHRISTOPHER BINGHAM of Pittsylvania County and CHARLES FOSTER, SR. In consideration of the premises and $1.00 conveys all his right, title and interest in said lands. CHRISTOPHER BINGHAM .

Last Will and Testament of NANCY NOAH dated September 1, 1881. To daughter COLUMBIA MOSS $1.00. All the rest of my estate to my husband, KING D. NOAH. Husband Executor. NANCY (X) NOAH. Witness: C. J. HARBOUR, WILLIAM W. MOIR. (Note attached to will from KING D. NOAH of Brim, NC dated June 6, 1902, stating that his wife died June 4, 1902, asking that the will be probated.)

Deed dated September 28, 1849 between DEBORAH HALL and DAVID McALEXANDER. In consideration of the love and affection for her children, DAVID T. HALL, JOHN R. HALL, MARY ANN HALL, MAHALA E. HALL and JAMES J. HALL and for the further consideration of $1.00 conveys 290 acres on the south side of Smith River known as the Fuson tract and also 1 bay horse, 7 cattle, 13 sheep, 32 hogs with increase, 1 clothe press, one beauro, 4 feather beds, 1 fall-leaf table and all household and kitchen furniture, present crops of corn, rye, oats, hay, fodder, wheat and plantation utensils. The said DAVID ALEXANDER will apply the profits to the discharge of debts which she now owes and that he will apply the income from the land and property to the raising and maintenance of said children after paying himself $85.07 and WILLIAM J. ROBERTSON $32.00. DEBORAH (X) HALL. Witness: WILLIAM J. ROBERTSON, ALEXANDER McALEXANDER, PETER M. McALEXANDER.

Deed dated December 3, 1813 between RICHERSON MAYO and BARNABAS BALISLE. Consideration of $60.00 conveys 50 acres on Buffalo Creek adjoining WILLIAM WARE and the little schoolhouse, WILLIAM BURNETT, SAMUEL HARRIS and NANCY HUGHES. RICHARDSON MAYO. Witness: JEREMIAH BURNETT, BENNET HOUCHINS, JACOB T. MAYO.

Deed dated November 15, 1815 between DAVID ROSS and JAMES SAUNDERS and JOHN RYAN. In consideration of $500.00 conveys 616 acres (this part missing). DAVID ROSS by his attorneys-in-fact, SAM BANKS, JOHN DUFFIELD. Acknowledged in Bedford County before WILLIAM R. JONES and CHARLES MARKLE, JR., Justices of the Peace.

Deed dated October 10, 1866 between LARKIN G. RUCKER and FANNIE OVERBY, infant daughter of THOMAS W. OVERBY. In consideration of a decree in the case of A. T. OVERBY'S Administrator against DIDY OVERBY, and in consideration of the premises conveys 120 acres, and being Lot #21 of the lands of A. T. OVERBY, deceased, on the waters of Peters Creek. L. G. RUCKER, Court Commissioner.

December Court, 1850 - A list of the property of COLTON B. SHORT, deceased, sold by FREDERICK SHELTON, Administration on November 7, 1850. Personal property list of purchasers included JAMES NOWLIN, JNO B. WILLIAMS, WILLIAM WITT, WILLIAM SHELTON, CARY CRAWFORD, JOHN RANGELEY, JAMES BOLING, JR., JOSEPH HALL, A. W.

BOLING, SR., JAMES M. CLARK, THOMAS HOPKINS, HUDSON SHELTON, CHRISTOPHER FOLEY and WILLIAM TOWNLEY for a total of $119.18. FREDERICK SHELTON, Administrator.

Deed of Gift dated March 10, 1835, between JOSEPH KELLY and GEORGE W. KELLY. Conveys 50 acres on Koger's Creek in consideration of his maintaining me for my lifetime and I give 1 cow and calf and 1 sow and 5 pigs, 3 beds and furniture, 1 table, 1 cubbard, 2 potts, 1 skillet and plantation tools. JOSEPH (X) KELLY, JAIN (X) KELLY. Witness: WILLIAM ARNOLD, ANDERSON (X) ARNOLD.

Bill of Sale dated November 14, 1834 between JOSHUA HAYNES, SR. and PHEBE HAYNES, his wife. In consideration of $115.00 paid by RICHARD HAYNES conveys 1 negro girl, Lucy, the remainder of which is after the death of JOSHUA HAYNES, SR. deed to PHEBY HAYNES to have and to hold the negro girl and the future increase of the same to the only use and behalf of RICHARD HAYNES. JOSHUA HAYNES, PHEBY HAYNES. Witness: MARTIN CLOUD.

To P. W. SHELORE, Judge - Pursuant to a deed of trust executed to me as Trustee by THOMAS D. RORRER for the benefit of CY HARBOUR dated November 3, 1888, I did sell the land to LOUISA McKENZIE for $963.89 and also another tract for $262.20. January 24, 1889. A. J. HARBOUR, Trustee.

Title Bond - Know all men by these presents, that I, THOMAS D. HOWELL, am held and firmly bound unto NANCY M. GOWING in the sum of $100.00. The consideration of said obligation is that NANCY W. GOWING has bought a certain tract of land at the price of $1.50 per acre, subject to Howell's right to a reasonable use of timber off the land. T. D. HOWELL. Teste: M.D. CARTER October 15, 1868.

Deed dated January 12, 1871 between WILLIAM TUDER and JOYCY TUDER, his wife, and PETER HAIRSTON. In consideration of $100.00 conveys 50 acres on the headwaters of North Mayo, south side of Bull Mountain, Goblintown Creek and WILLIAM LACKEY. WILLIAM TUDER, JOYCY (X) TUDER. Acknowledged before H. H. HALL, Justice of the Peace.

Deed dated September 24, 1830, between JOHN FERGERSON and THOMAS DeHART and JESSE DeHART. Whereas, Fergerson is indebted to THOMAS DeHART in the sum of $157.77 and being desirous to secure said debt, in consideration of $1.00 conveys to JESSE DeHART, Trustee, a tract of land on Rock Castle Creek, adjoining JOHN WILLIS, JOHN TUGGLE. JOHN FERGERSON, JESSE DeHART. Witness: ELIJAH DeHART, SR., JOHN DeHART, CHARLES DeHART, JOHN TUGGLE, AARON DeHART.

Deed of Gift between JOSEPH KELLY and WILLIAM ARNOLD. Conveys 25 acres on the waters of Koger's Creek together with the old cabbin which belongs to me for the consideration of $25.00. October 10, 1835. JOSEPH (X) KELLY, JAIN (X) KELLY. Witness: ANDERSON (X) ARNOLD, ANDREW ARNOLD, JOHN CHERRY, GEORGE W. (X)

KELLY.

Whereas, CHARLES HILL stands indebted to J. P. CARTER in the sum of $56.42-1/2 and is desirous of securing said debt, this deed made March 1, 1849 between CHARLES HILL and JEREMIAH B. TUGGLE, Trustee, and JOHN P. CARTER. In consideration of $1.00 conveys land on Blackberry Creek which was conveyed to him by his father, JOHN HILL, adjoining JAMES HARRIS and WILLIAM HILL. CHARLES (X) HILL, JOHN P. CARTER. Witness: J. W. CARTER, WILLIAM TINNY.

Deed dated June 30, 1828, between HAMON CRITZ, SR. and GABRIEL CRITZ. Consideration of $1.00 per acre conveys 25 acres on Spoon Creek taking in the house track, adjoining Murphy heirs. HAMON (X) CRITZ, SR. Witness: JOSEPH M. (X) AYRES, JAMES (X) ACRES, JOHN (X) SHELTON.

Deed dated September 14, 1788 between JOHN PRESTON of Henry County and JOHN SIMMONS of same. Consideration of 100 pounds conveys 100 acres on the branches of Mayo in Henry County called the Roundabout adjoining MICAEL LITTRALE. JOHN (X) PRESTON. Witness: JACOB ADAMS, JR., JOHN FLETCHER, JACOB (X) ADAMS. Proved January 12, 1789 in Henry County Court. Teste: JOHN COSS, Clerk.

Deed dated September 10, 1881 between A. M. LYBROOK, Commissioner, to SAMUEL D. POOR. In consideration of $660.00 the purchase price in the case of MORGAN GOING v. WILLIAM DEATHERIDGE. Conveys 186 acres on Clark's Creek. A. M. LYBROOK, Commissioner.

Deed dated December 1, 1898 between C. C. RATLIFF and E. A. RATLIFF, his wife, and SCHOOL TRUSTEE OF SMITH RIVER SCHOOL DISTRICT. In consideration of their interest in public school, conveys 1/4 acre on waters of Cold Fork Creek to be used for public free school, and if it ceases to be used as such for 3 years in succession, it will revert back to owners. C.C. RATLIFF, E.A. (X) RATLIFF.

Whereas, S. A. HANDY in his lifetime sold a tract of land to S.E. HANDY for which he was paid in his lifetime, and whereas, S.A. HANDY died without conveying title, and whereas it has been decreed by the Court that J.M. HOOKER, Special Commissioner, convey said land to S.E. HANDY or any one he may designate.

Therefore this deed made June 4, 1899 between J. M. HOOKER, Special Commissioner, and LOUISA HANDY, wife of S.E. HANDY. In consideration of the premises conveys land on the waters of Rye Cove Creek. J. M. HOOKER, Special Commissioner. Acknowledged before C. R. MARTIN, Clerk.

RICHARD MURPHY, JR. - Account current with PRIOR TATUM, Guardian. Expenses $36.87. Cash received for hire of a negro girl for the year 1847 plus rent for oats $18.26. Balance due PRIOR TATUM, guardian of the heirs of JESSE MURPHY, JR. $18.26 for RICHARD MURPHY. December 23, 1848. J.G. LEE, GEORGE W. HYLTON, GEORGE PANNILL, Commissioners.

Deed dated June 11, 1887 between I. N. AKERS and JOHN A. HOOKER, Trustee. In trust to secure to S. R. AKERS and JOHN HOOKER upon his official bond as Treasurer of the County of Patrick conveys 2 tracts of land, 1 of which he lives upon containing 232 acres and the other adjoining SALLIE ARRINGTON containing 300 acres, and all of his personal property except an iron safe which was heretofore sold to C. R. MARTIN. I. N. AKERS.

Washington, D.C. September 19, 1916. Dear Madam: To establish your title to pension, it is necessary to prove the date and immediate cause of the soldier's death. The date and cause can be proven either by a verified transcript of the public record or by the affidavit of the doctor who attended him in his last illness, but a verified transcript is preferred. Respectfully, EDGAR T. GADDIS (note in pencil "Your recent application received and filed.")

Affidavit - Claim No. 930003 of SUSAN OSBORNE, widow of JOHN OSBORNE, who served in Co. F of the 11th Regiment of Pennsylvania Cav. (Rest of the form is blank. On the back is a note "For Dr. W.B. MOORE to fill and sign. MORGAN S. GOING."

Deed dated April 1, 1899 between WILLIAM MARTIN and PERMELIA A. MARTIN, his wife, and J. F. JAMERSON. In consideration of $100.00 payable on January 1, 1900, conveys all of their right, title and interest in 368 acres, the lands of JEFFERSON H. BRAMMER, deceased, on the waters of Puppy Creek adjoining S. H. TURNER, JEREMIAH TURNER, deceased, J.A. HALL, JOHN R. HALL. WILLIAM MARTIN, PERMELIA MARTIN. Acknowledged before CHARLES U. GROVE, Justice of the Peace.

Deed dated September 6, 1879 between SPENCER F. NOWLIN, attorney-in-fact for WILLIAM M. THOMPSON, WILY CAYWOOD and NANCY CAYWOOD, his wife, of Washington County, Virginia and J. WILLIAM DALTON. In consideration of $327.00 conveys 69 acres on Mathews Creek. S.F. NOWLIN, Attorney-in-Fact.

January 26,1901 Survey for WALLER H. MARTIN on the waters of North Mayo containing 5-1/4 acres adjoining JNO TAYLOR. EUGENE LEWIS.

Deed dated January 5, 1881 between JOSEPH HAMMITT of Kingston, Ulster County, New York and MARY C. HAMMITT, his wife, WILLIAM D. HAMMITT of Philadelphia, Pennsylvania and WINONA C. HAMMITT, his wife, and CHARLES K. HAMMITT and ELIZABETH MOORE, wife of SMITH E. MOORE, of Kingston, Ulster County, New York (Both grantors and grantees being the only heirs at law and next of kin of REV. JOSEPH HAMMITT, deceased). In consideration of $1.00 and the further consideration of certain interests in lands in the State of Kentucky, conveys 1/2 undivided interest in 1000 acres on Volunteer Gap Road and part of BENJAMIN CHAMBERS land, and in 1500 acres adjoining BENJAMIN CHAMBERS survey, and being part of a larger tract conveyed W. A. BALDWIN and WILLIAM R. KIRK by F.B. WIGFALL, MARY ASHTON WIGFALL and LUCY CHAMBERS by deeds dated June 21, 1869 and October 15, 1869. JOSEPH HAMMITT, MARY C. HAMMITT, WILLIAM D.

HAMMITT, WINONA D. HAMMITT. Witness: FRANK CRAVEN, WILLIAM H. GRAY, C. J. CLAY, HOWARD DOUGLAS, FREDERICK HARMAN.

Contract dated September 25, 1876 between MATILDA STAPLES (Colored), mother of M. IZORA STAPLES an infant 6 years of age, and W. B. RUCKER. That the said MATILDA STAPLES with the consent of the County Court has placed the said infant as apprentice with W. B. RUCKER, with him to dwell and serve until she attains 18 years of age.
The said MATILDA STAPLES doth promise that the said M. IZORA STAPLES will serve her master in all lawful business, and shall behave herself toward her master during her apprenticeship.
The said Rucker shall instruct and teach the said M. IZORA STAPLES in the art and mystery of a housekeeper and cook and will provide for her sufficient food, drink, lodging, etc. and will learn her to read and write. MATILDA (X) STAPLES, W. B. RUCKER. Witness: B.F. SMITH.

Deed of trust dated February 8, 1913, between W. B. TUGGLE and LUCY TUGGLE of Rockingham County and R. T. STONE of Rockingham County, and JAMES W. TALLEY of Rockingham County, to secure $379.00 to Talley conveys 68 acres as surveyed January 22, 1905 by T. G. TATUM. W. B. (X) TUGGLE, LUCY TUGGLE. Witness: R. D. SIMS.

Deed of trust dated May 22, 1916 between J. F. MITCHELL and ANNIE MITCHELL, his wife, and ROBERT MITCHELL, and W. C. LESTER, Trustee. To secure $678.11 to R. W. GEORGE conveys 85 acres as surveyed by GEORGE D. HUBBARD, County Surveyor, in the year 1913, and being the same land J. F. MITCHELL and ROBERT MITCHELL purchased from GEORGE W. MITCHELL'S Special Commissioner on the waters of Elk Creek. J. F. MITCHELL, ROBERT (X) MITCHELL. Witness: R. E. WOOLWINE.

Deed dated April 5, 1900, between P. W. SHELOR, Commissioner, and W. P. STAPLES. Whereas it was decreed in a suit entitled M. WEDDLE'S Complainants and J. L. OMARA'S defendants that G. D. HUBBARD should make sale of 90 acres of land adjoining PETER BELCHER, said Staples being the highest bidder at the sale. P. W. SHELOR, Commissioner.

Deed dated January 24, 1888 between JOHN RANGELEY and MARIA ANNETTE RANGELEY, his wife, JOHN F. NOEL and MARY NOEL, his wife, and HANNAH AYRES and JERRY SMITH. In consideration of $123.75 to be due by 3 installments, conveys 49 acres on Dan River adjoining J. H. ANDERSON'S line on Bee Branch. JOHN RANGELEY, MARIA A. RANGELEY, JOHN T. NOEL, HANNAH AYRES.

August 13, 1914 - To Honorable J. S. TAYLOR, Clerk. Sir - I executed a deed to H. H. HYLTON et als some time ago and I sent said deed by my son, GENERAL BERVEY HYLTON, commonly called "Doogie", and at the time I just sent you the deed for safekeeping and did not intend to acknowledge said deed. I was advised the day I executed the same that I could change the deed at any time. I don't want the deed recorded and don't want the deed to be considered as a good deed from me as I want to make a new one. EDMUND HYLTON (X). Witness: W. C. LESTER, R. E. LIGHT. I delivered the above deed for safekeeping and not to be recorded. G. B. HYLTON.

I have this day sold to L. G. RUCKER one house and 1/2 of the lot I bought of Mrs. PENCIA A. RANGELEY, being the upper half and all appurtenances, bounded by S. S. TURNER, for which L. G. RUCKER is to pay $250.00 in installments. December 6, 1892. J. E. PEDIGO.

Deed dated October 13, 1847 between ELIZABETH NICHOLS and FLEMING NICHOLS and WILLIAM TOWNLEY. In consideration of $25.00 convey all of their right, title and interest in 75 acres on Sycamore Creek and being the land CHRISTOPHER NICHOLS died possessed of, bounded by WILLIAM ROBERTSON, ROBERT WRIGHT and HYRAM D. WRIGHT, the interest of Elizabeth being 1/3 during her natural life and the interest of Fleming being 1/6. ELIZABETH (X) NICHOLS, FLEMING (X) NICHOLS. Witness: CRAWFORD TURNER, JAMES BOWLING, WILLIAM J. ROBERTSON.

Deed dated October 10, 1887 between C. E. SMITH and SALLIE SMITH, his wife, and W. B. SMITH. In consideration of a tract of land near the Town of Stuart valued at $500 and $125.00, conveys land on Russell Creek. C. E. SMITH, SALLIE SMITH .

Agreement date May 14, 1901 between J. F. TAYLOR and C. H. PUCKETT. Puckett agrees to furnish Taylor from time to time during the year 1901, goods, wares and merchandise and money not to exceed $20.00 for the cultivation of the soil and Puckett to have a lien on the crops to the extent of the advances. J. F. (X) TAYLOR, C. H. PUCKETT. Witness: KELSEY PUCKETT, CHARLIE TAYLOR.

It is hereby agreed between JOHN E. PENN and ROBERT CARTER, JOHN H. CARTER and JOSHUA J. CARTER that JOHN CARTER and JOSHUA CARTER are to cultivate the land of ROBERT CARTER at a rent of $30.00 per year payable on December 1 of each year to Penn to satisfy a judgment Penn has against ROBERT CARTER. ROBERT (X) CARTER, JOHN H. CARTER, J. J. CARTER June 5, 1878.

Surveyed from WALLER R. STAPLES to JIM RUCKER and GEORGE JOHNSON 63 acres on the north side of South Mayo River. December 30, 1875. M. T. LAWSON, Surveyor. WALLER R. STAPLES per JOHN E. PENN, his agent.

Agreement between LEE STAPLES and H. N. SIMPSON. Staples leases to Simpson a field on the opposite side of the river from Staples house to be sowed in oats this spring, known as the Cassell clearing. Simpson to furnish oats and pay Staples 1/4 of oats. March 15, 1873. LEE (X) STAPLES, H. N. SIMPSON. Teste: L. G. RUCKER.

By authority under a deed of trust executed by the heirs of JOHN P. WOOD, deceased, November 1, 1886, I did on January 29, 1887 sell to the highest bidder 766 acres by survey and 1/3 interest which Wood held in a 31 acre tract on the waters of Joint Crack Creek. J. F. TURNER and J. C. BARNARD became the joint purchasers for $1,603.00 of the 766 acres and ALEXANDER RAKES of the 1/3 interest for $5.00, and that he also sold the personal property for the sum of $459.24. January 29, 1887. S. H. WOOD, Trustee.

Agreement dated December 10, 1873 between JAMES RUCKER and GEORGE JOHNSON to conduct the farming business on certain field leased by Rucker from LEE STAPLES for the year 1874, to share equally in expenses and profits after expenses and rents are paid. JAMES (X) RUCKER, GEORGE (X) JOHNSON. Teste: L. G. RUCKER.

Deed of trust dated June 2, 1851 between MARTIN WEBB and JOHN CARROLL, Trustee. To indemnify JAMES H. HOUNCHELL and JAMES EARLY, securities for MARTIN WEBB with the Branch Bank at Wytheville of the Farmers Bank of Virginia in the sum of $300.00 doth grant land conveyed to Webb by JAMES WAUHOP on Lovings Creek and on both sides of Ward's Gap Road near the top of the mountain; and 2 sorrell mares, one 10 years old and one 5 years old; 8 cattle; 40 hogs; 8 sheep and all household and kitchen furniture, all crops and farming utensils. MARTIN (X) WEBB, JNO C. CARROLL. Teste: JOHN COCK, SR., W.C. CLEMENT, HENRY LANE, JOHN D. CHEATHAM.

Deed of Gift dated May 4, 1847, between THOMAS WILSON for the love and affection I have for my grandson, JAMES D. STANLEY and $1.00, conveys his blacksmith's tools, consisting of bellows, anvill, vise, tongs, and hammers. THOMAS WILSON. Witness: JESSE CORN, STEPHEN THOMAS.

Know all men by these presents that we CHESLEY RAKES and RICHARD THOMAS are bound unto JEREMIAH BURNETT, Executor of THOMAS TENISEN, deceased, for the sum of $180.00, the condition of said bond is that Rakes has received of JEREMIAH BURNETT $75.00, plus interest, in write of his wife's legacy left her by the last will of the deceased, and said Thomas has also received of Burnett $100.00. CHESLEY (X) RAKES, R. THOMAS. Witness: W.C. STAPLES, T.T. FLIPPEN. September 22, 1848.

Deed dated October 14, 1830 between WILLIAMSON SMITH of McMinn County, Tennessee, and RICHARD SIMPSON. In consideration of $50.00 conveys 50 acres on Johnson's Creek. WILLIAMSON SMITH. Witness: GAB. HANBY, H.H. MOORE.

Deed dated December 11, 1850 between SAMUEL G. STAPLES, ABRAM STAPLES, ALEXANDER A. MOIR and JAMES M. SMITH, Executor of JAMES M. REED, deceased, and DAVID RODGERS. Whereas, Rodgers in order to secure payment of certain debts did execute a deed of trust to SAMUEL G. STAPLES, Trustee, and did convey the interest which he acquired by his wife in the estate of ANDERSON ALLEN and whereas, a sufficient sum has been paid to release said interest, all claims to said interest are hereby released. SAMUEL G. STAPLES, A. STAPLES, A.A. MOIR.

Deed dated April 25, 1849 between JOHN H. TRENT and WILLIAM SPENCER, JR. In consideration of $100.00 conveys 45 acres on the headwaters of N. Mayo River adjoining THOMAS PENN. JOHN (X) TRENT, POLLY (X) TRENT.

Know all men by these presents that I, FRANCIS S. WIATT of Spottsylvania County, Virginia, attorney of HENRY O. MIDDLETON, for the consideration of $_____ do agree with JOHN CHAMBERS to convey _____ acres, being a part of a survey of 30,000 acres belonging to Middleton, it being patented in the name of HENRY LEE and once owned by JOHN M. RUSSELL and by him conveyed to Middleton. March 25, 1837. FRANCIS S. WIATT, Attorney of H. O. MIDDLETON .

Deed dated July 13, 1846 between JOHN CHERRY and CARRINGTON DILLION. In consideration of $20.00 conveys 22 acres on the north waters of Koger's Creek adjoining JOSEPH M. STOVALL. JOHN CHERRY. Witness: BRETT STOVALL, JOS. M. STOVALL, SALY STOVALL.

Deed dated _____, 1859, between HENRY HINES and JAMES H. HINES. Conveys 170-3/4 acres on both side of Peters Creek. (No consideration and no signatures.) Survey dated February 4, 1859 by JOHN H. KASEY attached. Bill for platting $5.00.

Deed dated May 26, 1883 between JOHN H. LAWSON and RUTH E. LAWSON, his wife, and WILLIAM P. PALMER. Consideration of $120.00 conveys 83-1/4 acres on the west side of Roan's Creek, a tributary of Little Dan River to the head of the ? and then with the hollow to the Westfield Road. JOHN H. LAWSON, RUTH E. LAWSON.

Deed dated May 17, 1843 between WILLIAM COMBS and WILLIAM DANIEL. In consideration of $120.00 conveys 120 acres on Falls Creek. WILLIAM COMBS Witness: THOMAS (X) COMBS, RICHARD HAYNES, JOHN ALLEN. (Subpoena issued for December 22, 1849 for THOMAS COMBS to appear and prove deed.)

Agreement dated September 6, 1873, between THOMAS DeHART and EDMUND TAYLOR that DeHart is to furnish Taylor with a house, firewood, water and garden spot free of rent, and a field near Mrs. Stovall's and one next to Mr. Jones for corn and one around the house for tobacco in return for which Taylor is to cultivate the crops and deliver 1/2 to DeHart. THOMAS (X) DeHART, EDMUND (X) TAYLOR. Witness: L. G. RUCKER, ASA WOOD.

Deed dated October 28, 1850, between ANDREW J. YOUNG and WILLIAM H. BUFORD, Trustee. Conveys all his household and kitchen furniture, his present crop of corn and tobacco to secure T.J. PENN, WILLIAM S. PENN, and HARRISON C. FRANCE $67.70, $83.80, $106.38, $51.90 and $20.00. ANDREW J. (X) YOUNG, WILLIAM H. BUFORD. Witness: JOSHUA E. WILLIAMS, HENRY C. McDONALD.

Deed dated August 6, 1802 between JOHN WALTER, SR. of Grayson County and SAMUEL TALBOT and JOHN A. GRIGG. In consideration of $500.00 conveys 500 acres on both side of Lovings Creek and 195 acres being part of a tract JOHN WALTER bought of HUGH ARMSTRONG down to Turner's line including the plantation and mill. JOHN WALTER. Witness: JOHN TALBOT, JOHN HIATT, JOHN (X) GRAYBEEL.

Deed of Trust dated September 9, 1852 between MUMFORD SMITH and JOHN C. CLARK. Conveys 150 acres adjoining WILLIAM MARSHALL, being the land where I now live, 1 horse, 3 cows and 1 calf, 7 hogs, 1 clock, 2 beds and household furniture, 1 shotgun, corn and tobacco crops to secure to THOMAS M. CLARK $46.14. MUMFORD SMITH, J.C. CLARK. Witness: J.A. HANBY. Notarized by SILAS CARTER, Justice of the Peace.

Deed dated March 4, 1848 between ROBBERT VIA, Executor of WILLIAM VIA, deceased, and JAMES FERGUSON of Floyd County. In consideration of $100.50 conveys 50 acres that WILLIAM VIA bought of DANIEL COX and wife on the south side of Smith River. R. VIA, Ex. of WILLIAM VIA, deceased.

Deed of Trust dated August 12, 1834 between JOHN BRYANT and NANCY BRYANT, his wife, and JOHN PLASTERS, Trustee, and IRA HURT of Franklin County. Whereas, Bryant is indebted to Hurt in the sum of $27.30 and to secure said debt conveys 40 acres on the waters of Goblintown Creek, and being the same land Bryant bought from JAMES HARRIS, and adjoining HUTSON ACRES, J.A. HAIRSTON, WILLIAM VIA. JOHN (X) BRYANT, NANCY BRIANT, J. PLASTERS. Witness: JOHN PARKER, A. MASSEY, FLEMING HANCOCK.

Deed dated July 16, 1825 between WILLIAM MURRY and PEGGY MURRY, his wife, and NANCY MORRIS, daughter of MILLY MORRIS. In consideration of $95.00 conveys 95 acres on Lovings Creek adjoining NEWMAN SIZEMORE. WILLIAM (X) MURRY, MARGARET (X) MURRY. Witness: JOSHUA HAYNES, ROBERT HAYNES, PLEASANT HAYNES.

I, SAMUEL HOWELL in obedience to an order of the Board of the Overseers of the Poor do hereby put a boy aged 15 years named ISHAM PUCKET unto JOHN BINGMAN until he arrives to the age of 21 to learn the art and mystery of distiling, during which time he shall serve his master faithfully, his secrets keep and his lawful commands obey. He shall not contract matrimony nor commit fornication, and he shall not bind or sell his master's goods without his master's knowledge; he shall not frequent ale houses nor play houses, nor follow any unlawful gaming during said term. JOHN BINGMAN shall provide sufficient lodging and clothing as shall keep him from intemperate weather and shall also teach him to read and write and cypher as far as the double rule of 3, and pay him his lawful freedom dues at the separation of the term of time. September 7, 1812. ISHAM PUCKET, JOHN BINGMAN. Witness: JAMES HOWEL.

Deed of trust dated October 18, 1812 between WILLIAM WARE and VALENTINE BURNETT. Whereas, Ware is indebted to BARNABAS BALIALS in the sum of $40 5 shillings and 8 pence, and in order to secure said debt conveys 1 feather bed and household furniture, 1 loom and its gin, 2 whals, 1 pare of cards, and 7 hogs. VALENTINE BURNETT, WILLIAM (X) WARE. Witness: JEREMIAH BURNETT, MARTHA (X) BURNETT, JEREMIAH (X) BELIALS.

Deed dated January 26, 1828 between RALPH J. MARTINDALE and ELIZABETH MARTINDALE and JOHN MARTINDALE. In consideration of $550.00 conveys 400 acres, a part of his father's tract, adjoining WILLIAM MARTINDALE, WILLIAM BURGE, and JOHN KING. RALPH MARTINDALE, ELIZABETH (X) MARTINDALE. Witness: WILLIAM MARTINDALE, GEORGE COLLINGS, JAMES COLLINGS.

Survey for WILLIAM SMART dated March 6, 1851 for 101 acres. JOHN KASEY.

Deed dated May 18, 1850 between HARDEN W. REYNOLDS, NANCY J. REYNOLDS and MOLLY VARNER, and ELIJAH H. WIMBISH, JACKSON PENN, JOSEPH KENNERLY, JR. and GEORGE C. DODSON, Trustee. Consideration of $1.00 conveys all right, title and interest which HARDEN W. REYNOLDS, NANCY J. REYNOLDS and MOLLY VARNER have in a one acre tract beginning at Hopkins' corner on the east side of the Courthouse road. That the Trustees shall build thereon a house of worship for the use of the members of the Methodist Episcopal Church South. H. W. REYNOLDS, NANCY J. REYNOLDS, MOLLY (X) VARNER. Witness: BENJAMIN WOOD, JOSEPH B. WIMBISH, WILLIAM L. MURPHEY.

Know all men by these presents that I, JOHN B. HATCHER, doth this day sell and convey my whole interest in the estate of JAMES HATCHER, deceased, to WILLIAM F. HALL for $30.00. May 7, 1849. JOHN B. (X) HATCHER. Witness: JOSEPH R. HALL, JOHN Y SHORTT.

Deed of trust dated December 19, 1821 between REUBEN COLLINGS and ANDREW JOYCE, Trustee, and WILLIAM BOYLES, JR. of Stokes County, North Carolina. Whereas Collings is indebted to Boyles for $25.00 and to secure said debt conveys 50 acres where Collings now lives and adjoining WILLIAM COLLINGS, SR., 1 cow, 1 heifer, 1 yearling, 8 hogs, tobacco, tools and household furniture. REUBEN (X) COLLINGS. Witness: EDM. OBRYAN, MOSES HIETT. (Assigned to JOHN FIELDS March 27, 1823)

Deed dated February 30(?), 1833 between STEPHEN HUBBARD, JOHN MASSEY and JAMES BARTLETT, Executors of JAMES BARTLETT, deceased, and JOHN AKERS, JR. In consideration of $400.00 conveys 83 acres on the north side of Smith River at the mouth of Widgeon Creek. JNO MASSEY, J. BARTLETT.

Deed dated September ____, 1832 between PAULINA KEATON and JOSHUA KEATON. In consideration of $1.00 conveys all her claim in the land conveyed by JOSHUA KEATON to PETER A. LEE, Trustee, and also in all personal property therein conveyed. PAULINA (X) KEATON. Witness: L.G. RUCKER, Deputy Clerk.

Deed of trust dated November 15, 1826 between GABRIEL DeHART and ELIJAH J. DeHART and ELIJAH DeHART. Whereas, GABRIEL DeHART is indebted to ELIJAH DeHART in the sum of $185.00 and being desirous of securing said debt, conveys to ELIJAH J. DeHART 213 acres on Joint Crack Creek. GABRIEL DeHART, ELIJAH J. DeHART. Witness: JESSE P. DeHART, CHARLES (X) DeHART, MARY (X) DeHART.

Deed of Trust dated March 6, 1824 between JOHN GUYNN and NATHANIEL McMILLION and WILLIAM AYRES. Whereas McMillion has this day entered himself as security for Guynn in the sum of $14.69 payable in good bar iron to JONATHAN UNTHANK 10 months from this day. Whereas, Guynn in order to secure said security conveys 15 hogs, 2 pots and 1 skillet, 5 earthen plates, 1 cotton wheel and 1 pair of cards, 1 water pail, 1 pig pen, 1 washing tub, 1 pale ax, 2 hoes and 1 plow, 1 handsaw, 1 file, 1 spike and chisel. JOHN GUIN, WILLIAM AYRES. Witness: JOSEPH McMILLIOND, JOHN McMILLOND.

Deed dated April 26, 1884 between JAMES R. ROBERSON and ELVIRA P. ROBERSON, his wife, WILLIAM G. ROBERSON and LUVELLA A. ROBERSON, his wife, and W. THOMAS BOWMAN. In consideration of $54.00 conveys 13-1/2 acres on the waters of the south fork of South Mayo River. J. R. ROBERSON, W. G. ROBERSON, LUVELLA A. (X) ROBERSON.

Deed dated August 13, 1887 between LEROY HENSDALE and CHRISTINA HENSDALE, his wife, and DAVID RAKES. In consideration of $200.00 conveys 33 acres on the headwaters of Little Dan, it being the same land Hensdale purchased from THOMAS C. PIGG and wife. LEE HENSDILL. CHRISTINA (X) HENSDALE.

Know all men by these presents that I, WILLIAM MARTIN, for the consideration of $85.00 paid by F. E. SMITH of Henry County, convey my entire crop raised in the year 1901, and 1 gray mare mule of the age of 8 years. March 25, 1901. WILLIAM (X) MARTIN. Witness: WALTER CLARK, ROBERT FOSTER. Acknowledged before JOHN H. CLARK, Justice of the Peace.

Deed dated February 20, 1899 between P. W. SHELOR, Commissioner in the suit of THOMAS SMITH et als v. BURWELL SMITH et als and HARRISON GOING. That whereas W.W. SPANGLER, Commissioner did make sale of the lands and HARRISON GOING became the purchaser for the sum of $255.00, and in consideration of said decree and the sum of $255.00 conveys 70 acres on the waters of Clark's Creek adjoining ELIA CONCIL and THOMAS DILLARD. P.W. SHELOR, Commissioner. Acknowledged before C.L. HARBOUR, Deputy Clerk.

November 27, 1867 - We the undersigned heirs of the estate of NANCY E. VIA, deceased, heir of the estate of JAMES VIA, deceased, doth this day give unto our mother, MARY VIA, widow of JAMES VIA, who is guardian for NANCY E. VIA, deceased, all our interest, right, and title in the estate of NANCY E. VIA, deceased, which amount was when received by our mother as guardian $320.00. Signed 1859. CHARLES J. VIA, WILLIAM P. VIA, JAMES E. VIA, MARY A. CONNER, E.D. VIA, GEORGE W. VIA, M.F. VIA, PENCIE McGRIFFIN.

Know all men by these presents that I, SAMUEL G. STAPLES, do hereby appoint ABRAM P. STAPLES, my attorney to sell a tract of land near the Town of Stuart devised to me by the last will of ABRAM STAPLES, deceased. Acknowledged before HENRY G. MULLINS, Commissioner in Chancery for Henry County. (No date).

Know all men by these presents that I, ABNER CAMPBELL, of

Frederick County, Maryland appoint W. R. WOOLWINE of Pearisburg, Giles County, Virginia, my attorney to sell and assign the right to use "Campbell's System of Indexing Records" in the counties of Floyd, Montgomery, Wythe, Franklin, Patrick and Grayson. April 19, 1881. A. CAMPBELL. Acknowledged before B. P. WATTS, Commissioner in Chancery for Giles County.

Deed dated January 2, 1864 between FRANCIS B. WEST and SOPHIA J. WEST, his wife, and JACOB SHELTON and SALLIE SHELTON, his wife, and JAMES RANGELEY. Whereas, some 3 or 4 years ago JACOB SHELTON sold the hereinafter described lands to FRANCIS B. WEST and made a deed to him which was lost and never recorded, and the said West failed to pay the purchase money and the said West thereafter sold it to the said Rangeley for $7.50 per acre and out of the purchase money Rangeley paid West's debt to Shelton.
In consideration of $412.50 conveys 50 acres a mile or so from the Courthouse in a northeasterly direction on the waters of South Mayo River adjoining W. L. McCANLESS. F.B. WEST, JACOB SHELTON, SALLY SHELTON. Acknowledged before JOSEPH MARTIN and THOMAS MARTIN, Justices of the Peace for Stokes County, North Carolina.

Deed dated July 25, 1879 between JOHN E. PENN, Commissioner in the case of JAMES TUGGLE and wife vs: WILLIAM THOMPSON'S heirs and NANCY THOMPSON and WILLIAM THOMPSON. In consideration of the decree in this cause conveys 69 acres known as Lot No. 2. JOHN E. PENN, Commissioner.

Memorandum of contract dated November 28, 1889 between WILLIAM A. BURWELL and JOSEPH T. PERKINS. Whereas Perkins having entered as surety for Burwell on an indemnifying bond to H. C. WOOLWINE as Constable to force a sale of property levied on at the attest of A. T. MITCHELL'S, to save him harmless from future risk has given this deed, that whenever it may become necessary for the protection of J. T. PERKINS as his surety, he is authorized to sell a lot of land at Patrick Springs which was reserved by the said Burwell in his deed to the company to whom COL. JNO E. PENN, his agent, sold the main tract. WILLIAM A. BURWELL, J. F. PERKINS. Witness: JOHN T. BISHOP.

Deed dated November 8, 1848, between DANIEL EPPERSON and JETHA EPPERSON, his wife, and ABIJAH McMILLION. In consideration of an exchange of lands and $225.00, conveys a tract of land on Clerk's Creek purchased from HARDEN H. MOORE adjoining JOHN KING. DANIEL EPPERSON. Witness: N.H. SCALES, WILLIAM EPPERSON, N.S. MOORE.

Deed dated September 5, 1840 between PERRIN JOYCE and ANDREW JOYCE. (No description and no consideration.) PERRIN JOYCE.

HENRY TUGGLE for C. PENN, Sheriff - 50 acres in the name of GEORGE ASKEW sold for non-payment of taxes. Purchaser, CONRAD PLASTERS. Amount of purchase money, 6 cents, the amount of the delinquent taxes. October 27, 1845.

Deed dated August 30, 1838 between JOHN A. HAIRSTON of

38

Yelleburke County, Mississippi, and JAMES VIA, SR. In consideration of $101.00 conveys 101 acres by recent survey on North Mayo and Blackberry Creek. JOHN A. HAIRSTON. Witness: WILLIAM H. CORN, JESSE CORN, JOHN (X) MARTIN.

Deed of trust dated December 20, 1843, between GEORGE W. KELLY, THOMAS J. PENN and GREENSVILLE PENN and PETER P. PENN, Trustee. Whereas Kelly is indebted to THOMAS J. PENN in the sum of $16.06 and to secure said debt conveys 40 acres on the waters of Koger's Creek adjoining JOSEPH STOVALL, WILLIAM ARNOLD and MARTIN DILLION and being the land on which JAMES KELLY now resides, and 1 sorrell mare, 2 potts, 2 beds and furniture and plantation tools. GEORGE W. KELLY, THOMAS J. PENN, GREENSVILLE PENN, P.P. PENN, Witness: M.G. STAPLES, ALEXANDER J. JOICE, WILLIAM D. HILL.

Deed dated August 18, 1848 between HUDSON SHELTON and LUCY SHELTON, his wife, and (rest of page blank except for signatures HUDSON (X) SHELTON, LUCY (X) SHELTON.) On back "Staples Trustee for Porter's children".

This day I will deliver to SEBEIRE(?) WEBB a parcel of land that JOHN B. WILLIAMS bought of JAMES M. REDD, bounded by HUDSON SHELTON and JAMES MURPHY and that I am bound to make the right as soon as I get in the bond that I gave to JAMES M. REDD for said land. January 1, 1838. J. B. WILLIAMS. Witness: GEORGE W. ADKIN, R.M. ZEIGLER.

I, JOHN H. TRENT, hath this day sold my part of the mill and land on Blackberry Creek to JOHN TRENT for $44.75 which may be discharged in horses, woole or leathers. November 27, 1827. JOHN H (X) TRENT. Witness: WILLIAM ARNOLD, NANCY EARLS, JNO G. LEE.

Deed dated January 11, 1836 between MARY CHAVERS and EDWARD LEWIS. In consideration of $15.00 conveys 25 acres on Smith River adjoining WILLIAM ROBERTS and PEYTON STANDLEY. MARY (X) CHAVERS. Witness: JOSEPH COX, ISHAM CRADDOCK, DRUSCILLA (X) LEWIS.

Deed of trust dated June 27, 1835 between FARTHING HIX and WILLIAM AYRES and WILLIAM SOWERS of Floyd County. Whereas, Hix is indebted to Sowers for $51.00 and to secure said debt conveys a tract of land on both sides of Rockcastle Creek known as N. Akers millplace including the old mill and adjoining JEFFERSON TAYLOR, ANDERSON TAYLOR, WILLIAM AYRES, and ISAAC ADAMS, it being the same land purchased of NATHANIEL AKERS. FARTHING HIX, WILLIAM AYRES, WILLIAM SOWERS. Witness: JOHN H. HIX, NANCY HIX, J. TAYLOR.

Deed dated September 5, 1794 between THOMAS POSEY and HARRISON HUBBARD. Consideration of 40 pounds conveys land on both sides of Smith River and Bowings Creek and Cow Branch. THOMAS POSEY. Witness: MOSSES GODARD, WILLIAM HEATH, JOHN SMALLMAN.

Deed dated April 23, 1877 between ANDREW KAMMERER of Philadelphia, Real Estate Agent, and CHRISTIANNA KAMMERER, his wife, and CHARLES W. COX of said city, Builder. In consideration of $3,180.00 conveys 320 acres adjoining JAMES TRUMTOWER on Volunteer Gap Road and being part of 950 acres. ANDREW KAMMERER, CHRISTIANA KAMMERER. Witness: SAMUEL L. ZAYLOR, GEORGE W. REED. Notarized in Philadelphia.

Articles of agreement dated July 10, 1865 between FOUNTAIN HOWELL and C. J. HERD and C.M. WIGGENGTON. In consideration of $25.00 leases to Herd and Wiggengton his old brick store in Taylorsville adjoining the dwelling house of A.A. MOIR and the Courthouse lot with the understanding that Herd and Wiggengton may give up the store at any time, paying only for the time they occupied same and also that they will give him possession at any time when he shall have made sale of same with 10 days notice in case of sale. FOUNTAIN HOWELL, C.J. HERD, C.M. WIGGENTON. Witness: L.G. RUCKER.

Deed of trust dated January 6, 1887 between WILLIAM C. MABE and A.J. BISHOP. To secure $110.00 to WILLIAM A. BURNETT conveys 74 acres on which Mabe now resides adjoining ISAAC MARTIN, said Mabe having been committed to jail in default of surety to appear in Danville at the next term of United State Court to answer a charge of violation of the revenue law as distiller, and to secure WILLIAM A. BURWELL as his security. WILLIAM C. (X) MABE.

Deed dated December 21, 1849 between G. ROSINBAUM, SAMUEL A. ROSS and JAMES ROSS and RICHARD HARBOUR. Whereas Rosinbaum was appointed Commissioner in the cause of Rosenbaum and wife against CHARLES L. FOSTER to convey the lands mentioned therein to the said Samuel A. Ross and James Ross, and they having sold the lands to RICHARD HARBOUR and do hereby convey 200 acres on the north fork of Goblintown Creek adjoining LEWIS FOSTER, JOHN KOGER, Carter heirs, and THOMAS HANCOCK (reserving the powder mill to CHARLES FOSTER). G. ROSENBAUM, Commissioner, SAMUEL A. ROSS, JAMES M. ROSS. Witness: E.B. TURNER, R.F. MOIR, THOMAS DeHART.

Know all men by these presents that we, RUTH MURPHY and WILLIAM F. MURPHY appoint JOSHUA E. WILLIAMS our attorney to receive any thing due us as heirs of JESSE MURPHEY, JR., deceased. May 20, 1858. RUTH (X) MURPHEY, WILLIAM F. (X) MURPHEY.

I have rented to HANNIBAL SIMPSON for and during a period of 2 years commencing on January 1, 1875, that portion of my farm known as the "Midals Shift" including dwelling homes, stables, corn cribs, reserving to myself the old garden attached to the overseer's home. Simpson hereby binds himself to seed all the land now growing in crops except the lots around the dwelling homes and stable and except that portion of the Red Level cleaned up and planted in corn during the present year; to cultivate the bottom on both side of the river and plant in corn, beans, and peas; to cultivate the lots around the dwelling homes, cabins and stables in tobacco. Staples will furnish fertilizer and 1/2 of the expenses of repairing the tobacco barns and fences and also the water gaps to protect the crops from stock; and whatever repairs are necessary. It is understood and agreed that for cleaning up the

Big Hill side overlooking the bottom on which wheat was grown this year, Simpson is to have the same rent free for 2 years. SAMUEL G. STAPLES, H. N. SIMPSON.

Deed of trust dated February 19, 1847 between MARTIN DILLION and WILLIAM H. BUFORD, Trustee, and T. J. PENN and WILLIAM S. PENN. Whereas Dillion is indebted to T.J. PENN and WILLIAM S. PENN in the sum of $107.23 and he being desirous of securing said debt, conveys his present crop of tobacco supposed to be about 3,000 pounds in the leaf. MARTIN (X) DILLION, WILLIAM H. BUFORD, T. J. & W. S. PENN. Witness: ALEXANDER SHOCKLEY, AUGUSTIN T. WEBB, JAS. PENN.

Articles of agreement between ANDERSON ALLEN and FRANKLIN HARRIS. Whereas Allen is the owner of the lands, tenements and waters of what is known as Yellow Sulphur Springs about 7 miles from Patrick Courthouse. Whereas, Harris is a citizen of Rockingham County, North Carolina, and has agreed with Allen to erect a cabbin on the lot where the said springs are situated for the benefit of his family. Harris is to have the privilege to cut timber and haul rock on said land to build said cabbin, and also a small cook kitchen near the cabbin and shall have the use of said cabbin for 7 years. September 8, 1847. ANDERSON ALLEN, FRANKLIN HARRIS. Witness: J.W. TAYLOR, EWEL DALTON.

I have received from CRAWFORD TURNER the sum of $1,400.00 he had in his hands as Sheriff that much of mine coming to my father upon executions he received and will not repay and from Jacob Black, he was unwilling to pay unless refunding bond was given, which my father refused to give, needing money, I have borrowed from Col. Turner the sum of $1,400.00 and executed my bond. I will pay him no interest unless he is made responsible for the same to some other person. November 31, 1882. W. R. STAPLES, C. TURNER.

This deed dated March 1, 1851 between JOHN B. WILLIAMS and JOHN HELMS of Floyd County. In consideration of $120.50 conveys 110 acres by recent survey on the waters of South Mayo River. J.B. WILLIAM. Witness: WILLIAM POTTER, SPARREL D. WILLIAMS, MEHALY BOULDIN .

Deed dated March 24, 1886 between R. J. WOOLWINE, Special Commissioner in the case of Janey and wife v. Thomas and others and THOMAS H. WHITLOCK. Conveys Lot No. 1 containing 149 acres and being the same land conveyed to said Whitlock by FLEMING JANEY, Commissioner for the heirs of SAMUEL BOYD, deceased. R. J. WOOLWINE, Special Commissioner.

In consideration of $30.00 HUGHS BROWN conveys to J. M. HOOKER, 1 bay horse named Bob being 5 or 6 years old. Hooker agrees to sell the property back to Brown on or before February 15, 1901 if Brown so desires, said property to remain on the premises of Brown until February 15, 1901 when he shall deliver same to Hooker. March 12, 1900. HUSE BROWN, J.M. HOOKER. Teste: T.J. TATUM. Acknowledged before T.A. TRENT, Deputy Clerk.

It is agreed between SAMUEL G. STAPLES and HAMILTON SIMPSON that Simpson is to occupy as a tenant for the year 1874 with the privilege of the present full work for the coming crop and also that part of the plantation known as "Middle Shift" embracing the cabins, stables, etc. except the meadow just below the graveyard. It is also understood that Simpson is to have the lands known as "Red Level" not cultivated last year free of rent upon cleaning up and cultivating it in either corn or tobacco. Simpson agrees that no one except the hands or their families are to occupy any of the cabins. November 27, 1873. SAMUEL G. STAPLES, H.N. SIMPSON.

Deed dated July 20, 1885 between SAMUEL H. HOGE, Commissioner in the case of D. G. HATCHER v. G.M. HATCHER and W.T. CLARK. In consideration of $225.00 conveys 220 acres by survey lying in Stokes County, North Carolina, and being the land allotted to JOHN C. CLARK and SUSAN CLARK, his wife, from the estate of DAVID B. HATCHER, deceased, beginning near the state line crossing Dan River, and Archie's Creek and adjoining state line. SAMUEL HOGE, Commissioner.

Deed of trust dated November 10, 1885 between H.C. LIGHT, J.T. HEARD, Trustee, of Henry County. To secure a debt of $83.70 to MOIR, SPENCER & BROWN conveys his entire crop of tobacco now in his possession made on his lands in 1885. H.C. LIGHT.

Know all men by these presents that we, RICHARD M. JOYCE and LEMUEL G. JOYCE, Administrators of JAMES JOYCE, deceased, JOHN A. ALLEN, GEORGE W. CORN in right of his wife, SUSAN JANE CORN, formerly SUSAN JANE ALLEN, and WILLIAM R. HOPKINS in right of his wife, SARAH A. HOPKINS, formerly SARAH A. ALLEN, heirs of CHARLES M. ALLEN, deceased, have entered into the following agreement: Whereas JAMES JOYCE was in his lifetime appointed guardian for the above named heirs and that certain moneys, goods and chattels came into his hands as guardian; whereas said Joyce paid unto SAMUEL G. STAPLES, receiver of the County Court $389.00 to the credit of CHARLES M. ALLEN'S children, and whereas the said children have arrived at the age of 21 years and the sum of money has not been paid to them, and they claim that amount against the administrators and in order to prevent litigation, it is agreed that said Administrators will pay the sum of $315.00 to be equally divided, on or before February 21 next. RICHARD M. JOYCE, L.G. JOYCE, J.A. ALLEN, GEORGE W. (X) CORN, WILLIAM R. (X) HOPKINS. Witness: L.G. RUCKER, FLEMING REYNOLDS. (No date). Filed with the Clerk December 21, 1876.

Deed dated June 4, 1899 between WILLIAM A. BURWELL, SR. and LUCY A. BURWELL. In consideration of the love and affection for his daughter conveys all his real estate including 21 acres known as the Patrick Springs property. WILLIAM A. BURWELL, SR. Acknowledged in Franklin County before C.S. SKAON, Notary Public.

Deed dated July 1, 1905 between C.P. NOLEN and JUDIE A. NOLEN, his wife, and GROVER BEAMER. In consideration of $100.00 conveys 12 acres on the south side of Smith River. C.P. NOLEN, JUDIE A.

NOLEN. Acknowledged before SPARRELL WOOD, Justice.

Deed dated September 16, 1795 between ANTHONY TITTLE and THOMAS W. RUBLE. In consideration of 75 pounds conveys 415 acres on both side of Goblintown Creek. (Part of deed missing). ANTHONY TITELE. Witness: DANIEL ROSS, LEWIS ROSS, ANN CRAFERD.

Articles of Agreement dated January 31, 1859 between SEPTEMUS BARTON and SAMUEL HOWELL and LARKEN G. RUCKER. That on January 4, 1858 Barton bought of Howell one house and lot in the village of Patrick Courthouse known as the Boyd lot, for which he was to pay $500.00 and gave a deed of trust on the house and lot and on a set of tiner's tools and all his household furniture; and that said Barton wishing to remove somewhere toward the west and wishing to carry with him all his household furniture, Howell consents that he may do so, and Barton agrees to give to L.G. RUCKER, Trustee, the tiner's tools to hold for the said debt until January 1, 1861 and hereby agrees to let the tools be used by the firms of Barton & Campbell at Patrick Courthouse until the 2 years is out. SEPTEMUS BARTON, SAMUEL HOWELL, L.G. RUCKER.

I have this day sold to L. G. RUCKER my house and lots on the Pike just beyond the lot of T. J. PENN where THOLES G. PENN built for the sum of $180.00 which sum is to be paid to THOMAS DeHART on a bond of $200.00 executed by JAMES T. SMITH and L.G. RUCKER, said lots supposed to contain 18 acres. Smith to convey the land to Rucker when said Rucker shall have taken up the bond from DeHart. March 23, 1882. J.T. SMITH

Commonwealth of Virginia - Governor's Office - March 11, 1882. L.G. RUCKER, Esquire Dear Sir I sent to Mr. Battershall deeds and other papers necessary to be executed by the parties at the North before we ever instituted suit, but have heard nothing from him for a year. Therefore, I do not know but he has abandoned the claim. I do not know whether the deed from Wigfall et als to Baldwin is worth recording without seeing it. In the meantime, I do not propose to move in the business and will thank you to remit the $7.50 I sent some time ago to pay for recording the deed. R.T. DANIEL, 101 W. Main Street.

Deed dated October 5, 1869 between T.B. WIGFALL and MARY ASTON WIGFALL, late MARY ASTON CHAMBERS, of Virginia and LUCY CHAMBERS of Chambersburg, Pennsylvania, and WILLIAM A. BALDWIN of Philadelphia, Pennsylvania. Consideration of $3,964.00 conveys 1/2 undivided interest in 7,492 acres on Johnson's and Wolf Creek (Chambers survey) adjoining North Carolina line. T.B. WIGFALL, MARY ASTON WIGFALL, LUCY CHAMBERS. Witness: WILLIAM H. SUTHERLAND, H. ALDERMAN. Acknowledged before J. HARTWELL ALDERMAN, Clerk of the County Court of Carroll County.

Deed dated May 27, 1850 between THOMAS KING of Stokes County, North Carolina, and GEORGE L. KING. Consideration of $300.00 conveys 25-1/4 acres on Elk Creek where Volunteer Road crosses same. THOMAS KING. Witness: G.H. ASHWORTH, JAMES N. TOLBERT,

HAMILTON JOYCE.

Deed dated January 7, 1881 between SAMUEL G. WALLER and JOSEPH H. WALKER. Consideration of $82.50 conveys 6 acres in Five Forks between the Tatum and Hines road. S.G. WALLER.

Deed dated March 4, 1890 between L.G. RUCKER and Z.T. ANGLIN and ADRON ANGLIN. In consideration of $5.00 conveys 38 square poles on Matthews Creek near the Anglin Trestle adjoining ROBERT CRITZ near the corner of the distillery. L.G. RUCKER, Z.T. ANGLIN.

Know all men by these presents that I have appointed W.W. MOIR my attorney to execute as surety for SAMUEL A. ANDERSON as Commissioner in the case of Gottschalk v. F.C. HAIRSTON, Administrator of P. W. HAIRSTON, deceased, a bond in the penalty of $9,000.00. October 6, 1887. S.G. WHITTLE. Acknowledged before JOHN H. MATTHEWS, Clerk of the County Court of Henry County.

Deed dated December 7, 1903 between WILLIAM BISHOP and T.J. BISHOP, his wife, and J.E. HUTCHINS. Consideration of $25.00 conveys 9 acres on Johnson's Creek. W.M. (X) BISHOP, T.J. BISHOP. Acknowledged in Carroll County before J.M. DAWSON, Justice of the Peace.

I have this day sold to Scales & Martin 30 barrels of corn now standing in my field to be gathered and hauled to them at my expense for the sum of $75.00. November 18, 1891. B.M. (X) McPEAK. Witness: P.W. SCALES, A.L. PANNELL.

Deed dated April 4, 1859 between JOSEPH KENNERLY, SR. and MARTHA A. ZENTMEYER, ELIZA A. HAIRSTON, GEORGE W. PENN, SARAH R. HAY, JOSEPH G. PENN, LUCINDA S. PENN, THOMAS G. PENN, WILLIAM A. PENN, and JOHN S. PENN, children and heirs of MARY C. PENN. Consideration of $75.00 paid by Capt. THOMAS PENN in his lifetime and also the natural love and affection he has for said children conveys 70 acres on the waters of North Mayo. JOSEPH KENNERLY. Acknowledged before JOHN R. COBB, Justice of the Peace.

Know all men by these presents that we, Z.T. DOBYNS and JOHN MERRITT have appointed P.W. SHELOR and JOHN R. MOORE our attorneys to execute before the Clerk of the Circuit court of Patrick County the several bonds required of us in the chancery suit Hylton & Harris v. ANDERSON McALEXANDER, J.P. PROFFETT, Adm, IRA P. DILLION, JAMES DILLION, Admr., and CALEB BOYD, Admr., in which Z.T. DOBYNS is the principal and JOHN MERRITT his surety and in the suit of MIDKIFF v. DAVID CONNER, Admr., et als. November 24, 1886. Z.T. DOBYNS, JOHN MERRITT. Acknowledged in Floyd County before B.S. PEDIGO.

Deed of Trust dated August 20, 1884 between ABRAM A. RORRER and CHARLES F. RORRER, Trustee, to secure a bond to MURRY TURNER and $25.00 due ISAAC JAMES for corn, and $10.44 due J.F. PERKINS, conveys my interest in the crop of corn and fodder now growing. ABRAM (X) RORRER.

This is to certify that I do authorize J.W. HOOKER to take out of the Clerk's Office a homestead deed lately filed by me for the benefit of myself. JOHN R. VIA. Teste: C.C. HOUCHINS.

Deed dated October 6, 1890 between C.J. HARBOUR and THOMAS K. WILLIAMS. Consideration $152.88 conveys 150 acres on Bull Mountain fork of South Mayo River adjoining PRESTON FAIN. C.J. HARBOUR.

Deed dated September 10, 1902 between J.H. BALISLE and JEANNETTIE BALISLE, his wife. Consideration of the premises and a new deed this day made to J.H. BALISLE by J.P. BOULDIN, JR., Commissioner, conveys to E.C. VAUGHAN all their right, title and claim to lands embraced in the deed of special commissioner to J.A. BALISLE dated October 20, 1892, and recorded in Deed Book 26, page 481, which by mistake was made to Balisle. J.H. BALILES, JEANNETTIE BALILES.

Deed of trust dated May 7, 1827 between SAMUEL MADCAFE and ELIZABETH MEDFEFE, mother of SAMUEL, and JOHN CASTLE, Trustee. SAMUEL MADCAFE is indebted to SAMUEL HOWELL in the sum of $7.50 and to secure the same conveys in trust 4 head of cattle; 1 black cow and calf; and 1 brindle cow and calf. ELIZABETH (X) MEDKEFE, SAMUEL (X) MEDFEFE, JOHN CASTLE. Teste: SAUNDERS WITT.

Deed dated January 22, 1901 between WILLIAM A. POORE and LUCINDA POORE, his wife, of Surry County, North Carolina and WILLIAM BISHOP. Consideration of $12.00 conveys 9 acres on Johnson's Creek adjoining JAMES SPARGER and JAMES MEREDITH. WILLIAM A. POORE, LUCINDA (X) POORE. Acknowledged in Surry County, North Carolina before S.A. TAYLOR, Justice of the Peace.

Deed dated June 17, 1901 between J.F. SOUDER of Greenbrier County, West Virginia, and JULIE SOUDER. Consideration of $42.50 conveys 17 acres adjoining Smith River, S.B. CHANEY, J.C. MARTIN, S.A. SOUDER, and EXONY SOUDER. Acknowledged in Fayette County, West Virginia before WILLIAM WARRICK, Justice of the peace.

Know all men by these presents that I CATY HANBY of Washington County, Virginia, do appoint my friend, WILLIAM CARTER, my attorney for me and in my name to claim any right of dower to all the lands formely belonging to my husband, JOHN HANBY, deceased. June 1, 1812. CATY HANBY. Teste: GABRIEL HANBY, NANCY CARTER.

I do hereby declare that I have never in my life at any time or place and under no circumstances charged JACOB McCRAW with any offence of an immoral character especially do I declare that I never charged him with any connection with a sheep as was alleged by EDMUND BEASLEY and I further declare that I did not use such language and it was false and without foundation. May 23, 1834. SEATON (X) CHANDLER. Witness: BARNABAS BALISLE, GEORGE W. KING.

This is to certify that in consideration of a request of WILLIAM GRIFFITH towards MEEKINS REYNOLDS and B. BALISLE as administrators for JESSE REYNOLDS, deceased, on a trust deed

45

executed to them and THOMAS REYNOLDS as Trustee, on all the said Griffith property.that is to say all of his household and kitchen furniture with all his stock and plantation utensils do crave that they sell the property whereon WILLIAM GRIFFITH now lives under the trust deed executed to them for the purpose of securing a debt which MEEKINS REYNOLDS and B. BALISLE is security to Col. GREENSVILLE PENN. I also give from under my hand that although the Trustee has not advertised the property for sale, I do consent to exonerate him from any responsibility in selling the land. WILLIAM (X) GRIFFITH, SUSANNAH (X) GRIFFITH, B. BALISLE, MEEKINS REYNOLDS. Witness: ROBERT TUDER, ISAAC (X) MARTIN.

Deed dated March 25, 1801 between PHILLIP BUZZARD and JOHN HUGHES. Consideration of $500.00 viz a bond from said Hughes to Buzzard for that amount and on the condition that Hughes is to keep Buzzard and furnish him with a plentiful supply of the necessities of life conveys by 2 surveys 581 acres on the north side of South Mayo River. PHILLIP (O) BUZZARD. Witness: PETER SCALES, RICHARD MILLS, HAMON CRITZ.

Deed of trust dated July 11, 1831 between GARDNER STEPHENS, GREENSVILLE PENN and GABRIEL PENN, Trustee. Stephens is indebted to GREENSVILLE PENN in the sum of $8.00 and to secure said debt conveys in trust the following, 1 black and white heifer and calf; 4 hogs; 1 bed and furniture, household and kitchen furniture; 2 axes; 1 hoe; 1 cotton wheel and 1 pair cotton cards. GARDNER (X) STEPHENS, GABRIEL PENN, GREENSVILLE PENN. Witness: P.P. PENN, GEORGE W. TAYLOR.

Know all men by these presents that I, SAMUEL CORN, of Franklin County, Tennessee, and held and firmly bound to JESSE CORN in the sum of 50 pounds, the condition of which is that SAMUEL CORN shall convey to JESSE CORN 50 acres, it being part of the land on which JESSE CORN now lives. November 1, 1823. SAMUEL CORN. Witness: RICHARD TURNER, JUDITH TURNER, NANCY CORN.

Deed dated August 21, 1798 between PETE HALE and SARY HALE, his wife, and SOLOMON JONES of Montgomery County. Consideration of 50 pounds conveys a tract of land on both sides of Puppy Creek containing 100 heakers adjoining WILLIAM PRICE, together with the plantation and all timber, utensils and belongings. PETER HALE, SARY (X) HALE. Witness: WILLIAM PRICE, B.M. PRICE, MARY PRICE, JOHN MANNIN.

Deed dated May 2, 1883 between Mc D. FOLY and BETTIE FOLY, his wife; SAMUEL W. FOLY and TEXAS FOLY, his wife, JAMES L. FOLY and BETTIE FOLY, his wife, ANDREW J. FOLY and MINTIE FOLY, his wife; and WILLIAM L. FOLEY, being the heirs of WESLEY FOLEY, deceased. Whereas the parties are desirous of conveying to each other the lands of decedent according to quantity and quality. In consideration of the premises and the sum of $64.00 to be paid to A.J. FOLEY, conveys 40 acres on Buffalo Creek. Mc D. FOLEY, BETTIE (X) FOLEY, S.W. FOLEY, TEXAS (X) FOLEY, JAMES L. FOLEY, BETTIE (X) FOLEY, A.J. FOLEY, MINTIE (X) FOLEY. Acknowledged before J.A.

BURNETT, Commissioner in Chancery.

A list of property bought at the sale of HARDIN H. MOORE by JACKSON SCALES on September 7, 1841: 4 beds and furniture, cubard, bearuo and book case, clock, 1 dozen chairs, 3 tables. Total $65.90 received from JACKSON SCALES. THOMAS M. CLARK.

Deed of trust dated April 15, 1830 between JOHN SHELTON and RICHARD STANLEY. In consideration of $12.00 owed to Stanley by Shelton, and to secure said debt, conveys his house tools and kitchen furniture, and the crops now depending of corn and tobacco. JOHN (X) SHELTON. Witness: JEREMIAH W. HYLTON, CONNER (X) MEGEHEE.

Deed from Mrs. ELIZABETH CLARK to J.P. CRITZ conveying timber on her dower land and also as guardian for her children. Also a deed from W. H. CLARK conveying timber on his land given to him by his father. I also have the right to locate my mills upon any of the above lands and to make all necessary road; that I wish to pay $1.00 per thousand for first clap box timber and $1.50 for second clap. (No signatures or date)

It is hereby agreed between JOHN E. PENN and GEORGE HAIRSTON that the said Hairston is to cultivate under the direction of Penn as much ground in corn as the said Hairston and his 2 sons can cultivate, said crop to be ploughed 3 times, and worked twice with the hoe. Penn to furnish horses and utensils and is to have 2/3 of the corn, fodder and shucks and George the other 1/3. George is to commence clearing the hill when Penn has commenced getting his winter's wood and may make as much as 1,000 pounds of tobacco, rent free. November 5, 1872. JNO E. PENN, GEORGE (X) HAIRSTON. Witness: JOSEPH (X) WIMBISH.

Copy of ROBERT POLLARD survey made July 4, 1795 on the waters of Dan and Ararat Rivers containing 65,000 acres now claimed by JOHN RANGELEY for non-payment of taxes adjoining JOHN MILLER, Buzzard Branch, Ararat River, R. MOORE, JOHN CREED, BETHENIA LITCHENS, Rentfro's Creek and the North Carolina line. November 19, 1852. M. T. LAWSON (THOMAS EPPERSON written on back cover.)

Inventory of the estate of WILLIAM H. FLEMING by WILLIAM FLEMING, Administrator. MARTIN CLOUD, SAMUEL GREENWOOD, S.J. SLUSHER, Appraisers. (No totals). Lists personal property and 2 bonds due by A.P FLEMING and SAMUEL W. BROWN. April Court, 1863.

Homestead deed dated March 18, 1871 by ARMISTEAD W. NEWMAN. Newman, a householder and head of a family, intending to avail himself of the homestead exemption, declares the following property: 1 undivided interest in land on both side of South Mayo formerly belonging to ELAM NEWMAN, household furniture, tools and farm animals, 2/3 interest in a cane mill, 1 due bill on JAMES M. TATUM, 1 due bill on ELAM NEWMAN and JOHN NEWMAN, 1 bond on JACOB S. CLARK. A.W. NEWMAN.

I have rented to LANDON DeSHAZO the house known as the West house and the garden surrounding it for the space of 12 months, for which DeShazo has entered into bond. January 13, 1876. GILDEROY (X) HALL.

A list of the sale of JESSEE MURPHY, JR., deceased. January 4, 1844. (Will Book 3, Page 269)

Deed dated January 15, 1801 between WILLIAM HICKENGBOTTOM of Washington County, Virginia, and JOHN WALTERS, JR. of Grayson County, Virginia. Whereas JACOB McCRAW granted to Hickengbottom on April 21, 1790, 100 acres on a branch of Lovings Creek. In consideration of $164.00 conveys said property to Walters. WILLIAM (X) HICKINGBOTTOM. Witness: JOHN WALLER, JAMES WALLER, SAMUEL CAREY, J. PARSONS.

Deed dated February 12, 1834 between ALEXANDER WHITE and PATSEY KITTY WHITE, his wife, and GREENVILLE WILLIS. Consideration of $25.00 convey all their right, title and interest in and to the lands of which JOSEPH WILLIS DIED SEIZED, it being 1/10 part of 393 acres. ALEXANDER WHITE, MARTHA (X) WHITE. Witness: JOHN WILLIS.

Know all men by these presents that I, NANCY GOWIN, for the love and affection I have for my granddaughter, EMBERSETTA HARRIS, convey 1 bed and furniture, 1 big wheel, 1 pott, 1 chest, and all other chattels and estate. December 14, 1829. NANCY (o) GOWING. Witness: JOHN MONDAY, WILLIAM B. VAWTER, ROBERT HARRIS.

Deed of lease dated December 10, 1873 between LEE STAPLES and JAMES RUCKER. Staples leases to Rucker for 1 year the field known as the Old Basin and the Castle Clearing south of Mayo River embracing a portion of the land cultivated in tobacco by JOHN BURWELL yielding on the part of said Rucker a rent of 10 barrels of corn for the Old Basin and 7 barrels of corn and a blade stack for the Castle clearing. LEE (X) STAPLES, JAMES (X) RUCKER. Witness: L. G. RUCKER.

Lease dated December 19, 1878 between THOMAS DeHART and HENRY WONDERLAND. DeHart has leased to Wonderland a part of his land known as the JAMES M. ROGERS place and DeHart agrees to furnish in addition to the land a mule to do the plowing and the tools to work the land and all necessary seeds, and to feed the mule and repair the tools and Wonderland agrees to cultivate the lands to the best of his ability and to deliver to DeHart at his homeplace 1/2 of everything he makes. THOS. DeHART (X), HENRY WONDERLAND (X).

Know all men by these presents that PRESTON HUGHS and WALKER T. NOEL are bound to LEE STAPLES in the amount of $73.00 payable on January 8, 1873, the condition of which is that Staples has sued out a warrant of distress against goods and chattels of PRESTON HUGHES and whereas, W. T. AKERS, Sheriff, has seized the following property of said Hughes, 1 lot of leaf tobacco, 1 yearling calf and 1 stack of blade fodder. The said Hughes being desirous of keeping the said property until next term of court has tendered WALKER T.

NOEL as his security for the deliverance of said property at next term of Court. PRESTON (X) HUGHES, W.T. NOEL.

Know all men by these presents that we, D. J. ROBERTSON and E. F. ROBERTSON, are bound to the Commonwealth for $200.00, the condition of which is that D. J. ROBERTSON has this day contracted with the County Court for the maintenance of M. F. ROBERTSON, a lunatic, according to the decision of 3 Justices, until he may be further dealt with. D. J. ROBERTSON, E.F. ROBERTSON. May 26, 1876.

Deed of Trust dated December 10, 1842 between SOLOMON WEAVER and JOHN WEAVER, and DANIEL WEAVER, Trustee. Whereas Solomon is indebted to John in the sum of $187.00 due June 20, 1838, and a due bill for $7.25 and a note for $12.75 and an account for $150.76, and being desirous of securing said debts conveys in trust 1 bay mare, 1 rone mare, 2 cows, a buffalo colt, 1 red cow, 1 pided cow, 1 yearling, 1 calf, 9 sheep, 25 hogs, 1 clock and all household and kitchen utensils. SOLOMON WEAVER, DANIEL WEAVER, JOHN WEAVER.

It is agreed between JAMES W. CAMPBELL and JAMES DALTON that Dalton is to have possession of a tract of land owned by Campbell and known as the Old WILLIAM CRITZ tract, for the year ending December 31, 1878, except the lot on which JAMES FITZGERALD lives. Dalton to cultivate said land and pay Campbell 1/4 of the crop. August 23, 1877. J.W. CAMPBELL, JAMES (X) DALTON.

I have this day sold to THOMAS T. DeHART a tract of land on South Mayo River embracing the land DANIEL HARRIS lives on and the land JAMES W. RODGERS lives on for $180.00, and I hereby bind myself to make a deed whenever the purchase money is put up. October 14, 1874. SAMUEL G. STAPLES.

Deed of trust dated April 4, 1835 between GEORGE PRILLAMAND and B.M. PRICE and JOHN LACKEY(?) and JOHN PLASTERS, JESSE CORN, JOHN HAIRSTON and JOHN TURNER, Commissioners. Whereas Prillamand and Price are indebted to the Commissioners in the sum of $250.50 and being desirous of securing said debt convey in trust 215 acres adjoining Anglin Falls and Smith River. GEORGE PRILLAMAN, B.M. PRICE, JR., J. PLASTERS, JESSE CORN, J. HAIRSTON, J. TURNER. Witness: T. WATKINS, WILLIAM SIMS, ROBERT T. HAIRSTON.

Deed of partition dated June 23, 1852, between ABRAM STAPLES and THOMAS M. CLARK. Whereas the parties have equal shares in several tracts of land, to-wit: 175 acres on Johnson's Creek, adjoining JOHN EATON and being bought at the sale of ANDERSON FOWLKES; 161 acres on Johnson Creek, adjoining MARTIN CLOUD and S. GREENWOOD, and also being purchased at said sale; 599 acres adjoining MARTIN CLOUD and being purchased at said sale. The parties do make the following partition, Staples to have 599 acres and Clark to have 175 acres and 161 acres as his part. A. STAPLES, THO. M. CLARK.

Deed dated April 18, 1812 between JAMES BROWN and SARAH BROWN, his wife, of Halifax County, and ALEXANDER BROWN of Pittsylvania County. Consideration of $400.00 conveys 498 acres on Hicks Fork on the waters of Dan River granted by patent to DAVID LAWSON and by him made over to ALEXANDER BURGE, and from him it was purchased by JAMES BROWN, adjoining JEREMIAH COLLINS. JAMES BROWN, SARY BROWN. Witness: P.R. GILMER, JAS. GARLAND, GEORGE WELLS.

Deed of trust dated March 20, 1830 between THOMAS SHARP, JOHN A. HAIRSTON and JESSE CORN. Whereas Sharp is indebted to Hairston in the sum of $97.00, and being desirous of securing said debts conveys to Corn in trust 194 acres on the waters of Mayo River adjoining BENJAMIN SPENCER, and MARY ANN WATSON. THOS. SHARP, J.A. HAIRSTON, JESSE CORN. Witness: L. P. STOVALL.

Deed dated May 23, 1803 between HUGH ARMSTRONG of Surry County, North Carolina, attorney for WILLIAM ARMSTRONG of Hawkins County, Tennessee, and JOHN ARMSTRONG. Consideration of $1,400.00 conveys 1050 acres adjoining JOHN BROWN. HUGH ARMSTRONG, Attorney in Fact for WILLIAM ARMSTRONG. Witness: CHARLES BURRIS, JAS. KINCANNON, JR., JAMES (X) HENDERSON.

Know all men by these presents that I, ADAM LINVEL FOLEY, of Henderson County, Tennessee, appoint L.G. RUCKER my attorney to close up and settle with my guardian, WILLIAM WITT, concerning the matter of his guardian ship of myself, and to receive any sum coming to me from said guardian. January 21, 1877. A.L. (X) FOLEY. Witness: H.M.C. WEBB, JAS. A. HENRY. Acknowledged in Henderson County, Tennessee, before ISAAC T. BELL, Circuit Court Clerk.

Deed dated January 19, 1878 between JAMES A. PENN and LUCINDA PENN, his wife, of Forsythe County, North Carolina, and JOHN G. STAPLES, of Rockingham County, North Carolina. Whereas, JAMES PENN sold to WILLIAM C. STAPLES 140 acres on Green Creek and WILLIAM STAPLES did transfer it to said JOHN G. STAPLES. Consideration of $2,200.00 conveys 141 acres. J.A. PENN. Acknowledged before WILLIAM C. STAPLES, Notary Public for Rockingham, County, North Carolina.

Deed dated May 8, 1899 between S.C. SCOTT and E. P. BARNARD, Trustee. Consideration of $350.00 conveys 82-1/2 acres on the waters of Round Meadow Creek adjoining THOMAS SCOTT, to save harmless J.H. COCK and E. McALEXANDER, securities for S.C. SCOTT to the People's Bank. S.C. SCOTT. Acknowledged before J.N.T. BARNARD, Justice of the Peace.

Homestead deed dated May 31, 1881 by R.H. HALL claiming homestead exemption to 610 acres of land on Arches Creek and various items of personal property and farm animals for a total of $1,322.75. R.H. HALL .

Know all men by these presents that I, S.J. COOK, appoint JAMES H. MARTIN my attorney to sign my name as security for S. P. RUCKER as Administratrix for GEORGE M. RUCKER, deceased. August

26, 1884. S.J. COOK. Witness: H.S. SLAYDON. Acknowledged in Henry County before J.T. GRAVELY, Notary Public.

We hereby sell to JOSHUA KEATON our interest in 25 acres on the head branches of North Mayo River and Spoon Creek owned by our deceased father, ELIJAH SPENCER. September 15, 1855. HARDIN R. (X) SPENCER, ALFORD (X) SHOUGH, LUCINDA(X) SHOUGH. Witness: WILLIAM AYRES, DANIEL R. PEDIGO.

Deed of Gift dated September 6, 1854, between CHARLES T. MARTIN and AGNES MARTIN, his wife, and JOHN H. MARTIN. Consideration of $1.00 conveys 102 acres on the southwest side of the road leading from the five forks to HENRY HINE'S line, known as part of the Brown tract formerly owned by SAMUEL STAPLES, deceased, and devised by him to his daughter, RUTH P. STAPLES, who intermarried with JAMES M. REDD, deceased, and then conveyed by RUTH P. REDD and the heirs of JAMES M. REDD to CHARLES T. MARTIN. CHARLES T. MARTIN, AGNES MARTIN. (Deed Book 15, page 92).

Deed dated July 29, 1866 between JOHN GUNTER and JOSEPH H. GUNTER, GEORGE B. GUNTER and JOHN W. GUNTER. Love and affection for his sons and in the further consideration that he is old and feeble in health and is chiefly dependent on his children for the support of himself and his wife, he gives all his right and title to his hometract of land containing 150 acres lying on the waters of Peters Creek, adjoining ALLEN T. MITCHELL, and also 1 black mare about 12 years old, and all his personal property, tools and crops. JOHN GUNTER.

Deed of trust dated August 7, 1867 between RICHARD COCKRAM and J.T. CLARK, Trustee. Cockram grants in trust to Clark 3 oat stacks, interest in corn now growing, interest in all brandy to be made from fruit on the place he is now tending, 2 yearlings, hogs, and 1 man's saddle, to secure MURRY TURNER in the sums of $9.00 and $21.50. RICHARD COCKRAM, J.T. CLARK.

Deed of homestead dated December 26, 1870 by JOHN SHELTON, a householder and head of a family, intending to avail himself of the homestead exemption declare the following: 24 acres lying in the rough and known as the place settled by W.W. DOSS purchased of SAMUEL G. STAPLES for $240.00, which has not been paid, household property and crops. Total $326.78. JOHN (X) SHELTON.

J.A. ROSS, Trustee on a deed of trust executed by JAMES A. EANS on June 8, 1885, to indemnify C.P. NOLEN, J.A. NOLEN and W.L. HALL, surety for Eans, and Eans having failed to pay said debts, and being required by sureties to sell the lands, did so on May 16, 1891. J.A. NOLEN, C.P. NOLEN and W.L. HALL being the highest bidders at the price of $400.00, and I have accounted for and disbursed said funds. May 20, 1891. J.A. ROSS, Trustee.

Deed dated August 28, 1882, between DALLAS PENN "colored" and VALENTINE HYLTON, "Trustee. Penn conveys in trust to Hylton all his crops, household and kitchen furniture and 3 hogs to secure a note to J.P. CRITZ for $120.65 and a note for $100.00 (this note being given for the purchase of a mouse colored horse mule named "George", the right of property remains with Critz until the note is paid.) DALLAS (X) PENN. Witness: M.D. GREGG, R.L. PENN.

It is hereby agreed between WILLIAM F. MURPHY and SUSAN L. PENN that Murphy is to pay Penn $50.00 for her clay-bank horse, payable in work before December 25, 1881. September 26, 1881. WILLIAM F. MURPHY (X), SUSAN L. PENN, JNO E. PENN.

List of heirs of J.L. SALMONS, deceased: I. J. SALMONS, 43, Woolwine, Va; SALINE L. P. WOOD, 41, Floyd, Va; LANDON P. SALMONS, 40, Floyd, Va; WILLIAM C. SALMONS 36, Woolwine, Va; MARY L. SMITH 34, Woolwine, Va; AMOS J. SALMONS, 32, Woolwine, Va. LATHENA B. (X) SALMONS. May 17, 1913. J.H. DILLON, Justice of the Peace.

Annual report of WILLIAM B. SMITH, Superintendent of the Poor of Patrick County December 4, 1871. The following persons were in the poorhouse: JOSEPH HARRIS; SALLY PARR; CHARLOTTE PARR and her child, HENRY PARR, about 2 years old; REBECCA MURPHY and her 3 children, THOMAS MURPHY and ZACK MURPHY (twins) about 2-1/2 and ADDA MURPHY about 7 months; BETSY WILLARD and her child ABE WILLARD, about 2 years old; SUSAN EDWARDS, an idiot; JANE HICKS and her child, MANDA HICKS, about 1-1/2; BETSY RUCK and her child about 2 months old, not named; KATHERINE WADE and her children, ALICE WADE about 15 months, and HENRIETTA WADE about 5 years; MARTHA ADAMS and her child, a girl about 1 year; LUCINDA CARTER (colored); HANNAH SMITH (colored); LAURA G. ROBERTSON 5 or 6 years (colored); JAMES WILLARD, a boy about 4 years old; FRANCES TUGGLE.

Title bond dated March 20, 1890 between R.J. BOYD and ROBERT BOYD. I, R.J. BOYD, do sell my interest in 78 acres known as the Bowman land owned by MAZY BOYD now, on the waters of Johnson's Creek, adjoining J.C. YOUNG and ROBERT MARSHALL, for $25.00 paid in advance, and do bind myself to make a deed. R.J. BOYD. Witness: JAMES H. SMITH, C.J. COLDMOND.

Deed dated June 5, 1909 between MARY A. CRUISE, the widow of JAMES CRUISE, deceased, S.H. WOOD and MINDA WOOD, his wife; JOHN W. WOOD and NANIE WOOD, his wife; GERMAN B. WOOD and RILLA WOOD, his wife; JAMES H. WOOD and ROSY WOOD, his wife; R.V. WOOD and BERTHA WOOD, his wife; J.S. WOOD and MARTHA WOOD, his wife, NANCY HALL and GREEN HALL, her husband; ADA HARRIS and CHARLIE HARRIS, her husband, the heirs of ELIZABETH WOOD, deceased, and J. D. CRUISE. Whereas, in the year 1870, JOSEPH H. HELM bought of S.H. WOOD and ELIZABETH WOOD, his wife, 100 acres known as the JAMES CRUISE, deceased, land; and whereas, there never being a deed executed to Helm and the said Helm sold the same to J.D. CRUISE and there never being a deed made to Cruise. Wherefore, the above parties join in this deed to convey all their right, title and interest in the lands lying on the waters of Smith and Dan Rivers. MARY A (X) CRUISE, W.H. WOOD, J.W. WOOD, NANNIE WOOD, J.H. WOOD, ROSA WOOD, J.S. WOOD, M.C. WOOD, R.V. WOOD, BERTHA WOOD, GERMAN B. WOOD, RILLA WOOD, NANCY HALL, GREEN (X) HALL, ADA HARRIS, CHARLIE C. HARRIS.

Acknowledged before WILLIAM M. UNDERWOOD, Justice of the Peace.

Deed dated September 10, 1904, between JOSEPH TUGGLE and STACY M. DUNCAN. Consideration of $25.00 conveys 12 acres on the waters of Squirrel Creek, adjoining Spice Cove. JOSEPH (X) TUGGLE. Witness: J.D. REYNOLDS.

Satisfaction of a deed of trust dated March 20, 1897 executed by W.L. KING, G.B. KING to The Aultman and Taylor Machinery Company. April 10, 1897.

Know all men by these presents that I, GEORGE W. LAURENCE, being justly indebted to Martin & Nelson of Stokes County, North Carolina, in the sum of $200.00, and being desirous of securing said debt do hereby convey the following: 1,000 pounds of leaf tobacco, and 20 barrels of corn. G.W. LAURENCE. Witness: V. HYLTON, A.J. BROWN, W.R. JOYCE. ____, 1872.

Deed dated December 30, 1870 between GREEN R. CONNER, Trustee, WILLIAM MORAN, CHARLIE DeHART and HENRY TUGGLE. Whereas, Moran in order to secure notes to Tuggle and DeHart did convey in trust to Conner all his lands and certain personal property, and now said debts have been paid and all property is released to Moran. (No signatures)

Deed dated October 10, 1845, between JOHN LIGHT and JAMES LIGHT and SAMUEL HOWELL. Consideration of $50.00 conveys 30 acres on South Mayo River. JOHN G. LIGHT, JAMES LIGHT. Witness: WILLIAM (X) VIPPERMAN, TOMLAIN HOWELL.

Deed dated January 8, 1803 between DAVID McGOWN and DAVID QUARLES. Consideration of 100 pounds conveys 114 acres on Johnson's Creek. DAVID McGOWN, SARAH McGOWN. Witness: JAMES DICKENSON, THOMAS BRANSON, ELIHU AYERS.

Deed dated November 16, 1795, between GEORGE TITTLE and JOSEPH HALE, SR. Consideration of 50 pounds conveys 59 acres on Goblintown Creek. GORGE (X) TITTLE. Witness: A. TOM TITTLE, ANTHONY TITTLE, DAVID TITTLE.

Deed dated November 18, 1836 between WILLIAM PICKEREL and MILTON R. DODSON. Consideration of $200.00 conveys 100 acres on Russell's Creek, it being the land Pickerel purchased from SAMUEL SHARP. WILLIAM (X) PICKEREL. Witness: M.L. CLARK, JOHN (X) GRADY, HENRY H. (X) ALVIS.

List of personal property of JOHN W. BRAMMER, deceased, on May 15, 1868. 1 bond on WILLIAM LYON, JR., M.L. HOUCHINS, RICHARD HATCHER, W.H. DAVIS, GEORGE R. ROGERS, PETER CASSELL, G.C. EARLS, BRADLEY MEREDITH, DAVID WASHINGTON, W.R. AYERS, NICHOLAS CURATHO, JOHN ALEXANDER, WILLIAM McGEE, J.H. DeHART, A. ADAMS, FRANCIS AYERS, WILLIAM HUBBARD, JOHN BELCHER, ROBERT DeHART, GABRIEL DeHART, C.J. DILLON, THOMAS H. KOGER. Items of personal property. WILLIAM DILLON, JOHN LEE, J.A. TAYLOR, Appraisers. CALEB BOYD,

Administrator.

Deed dated September 18, 1805 between LARKEN PRICE and WILLIAM PRICE. Consideration of 5 shillings leases the hole of the land and plantation whereon WILLIAM PRICE now resides for and during the life of the said William and his wife, MARRY PRICE. LARKEN PRICE. Witness: WILLIAM PRICE, BARNARD M. PRICE, JAMES LEWIS .

Deed dated January 16, 1833 between BARNABAS BALISLES and the Legatees of JESSE REYNOLDS, SR., deceased. In consideration of $201.50 paid to JESSE REYNOLDS, JR. and MALINDAY REYNOLDS, his wife; MEEKINS REYNOLDS and MARY REYNOLDS, his wife; THOMAS MORRISON and JINEY MORRISON, his wife; WILLIAM GRIFFITH and SUSANNAH GRIFFITH, his wife; JOHN A. NUNN and LEVINAH NUNN, his wife; THOMAS LAWLESS and FRANCIS LAWLESS, his wife; JAMES ADAMS and ONEY ADAMS, his wife, GEORGE REYNOLDS, MACAJAH MARTIN and SELEY MARTIN, his wife, conveys 221 acres. WILLIAM (X) GRIFFITH, MEEKINS REYNOLDS, MICAJAH (X) MARTIN, THOMAS (X) LAWLESS, JESSE REYNOLDS, JR., GEORGE REYNOLDS, THOMAS MORISON. Witness: F(T?) WEBB, GEORGE REYNOLDS, DANIEL GRAY, WILLIAM CRITZ, JOHN TUGGLE, PAUL C. INGRUM, GERMAN KEATON, JORDAN (X) KEATON, GEORGE (X) BALISLE.

Deed dated December 3, 1881 between ELIZABETH HOWELL, BLUFORD McPEAK and SARAH McPEAK, his wife; HENRY FAIN and LOUISA J. FAIN, his wife; MOLLY HOWELL, SAMUEL J. LIGHT and EMBERZETTA LIGHT, his wife; PETER CRUISE and TEXAS CRUISE, his wife; MELIA HOWELL and SARAH A. RORRER, widow of JOHN H. RORRER, A.J. RORRER and J.W. RORRER. Consideration of $30.00 conveys 50 acres on the waters of South Mayo River in Goings Mountain adjoining the north side of WILLIAM A. BURWELL'S, now THOMAS D. RORRER, known as the Meadow Place, RICHARD FARIS, JR., PAUL HOWELL and the Old Poorhouse. HENRY (X) FAIN, LOUISA J. FAIN, PER MELLA HOWELL.

Deed of lease dated February 2, 1822 between ARTHUR GARVEN and PAUL ELGAN. Consideration of $60.00 conveys 100 acres on Smith River for the term of 10 years, adjoining JOHN LEWIS, JOHN CONNER and SAMUEL C. MORRIS. ARTHUR GARVEN. Witness: JOHN ELGAN, E. HARRIS, JAMES BURNETT.

Deed dated December 13, 1847 between AARON DeHART, JAMES REYNOLDS and WILLIAM SPENCER (Rockcastle), WILLIAM J. ROBINSON, SAMUEL McALEXANDER and PERRY GRAHAM. Whereas, by deed dated April 19, 1843 made by JAMES REYNOLDS, AARON DeHART and the said Spencer, et als, in consideration of $76.16, $57.00, $498.78 did grant to AARON DeHART 165 acres on Rockcastle Creek, it being the same land purchased by JAMES REYNOLDS from JOHN TUGGLE; 350 acres adjoining, on both side of Rockcastle, it being the same tract where Reynolds now resides; 130 acres on Rockcastle, it being the land Reynolds purchased from CATHERINE HEFFLEFINGER, and the following person property in trust: 1 negro man slave named DAVID, age 42; 1 negro slave NANCY, about 30 years old; 1 negro boy CREED about 1 year old; 1 negro boy GREEN, about 16 years old; 1 negro girl TAMSEY, about 8 years old; 1 negro boy ABRAM, about 4 years old; 5 horses, 1 yoke of oxen and cart, household furniture and kitchen utensils, now in the possession of Reynolds, 3 bee stands, 4 saddles, 800 pounds of bacon; 20 bushels of corn; 2 shot guns, 2 rifles, and all the interest Reynolds may have in the estate of WILLIAM PERKINS, deceased, by virtue of a purchase from the children of WILLIAM BOYD now in suit in the Superior Court of Patrick; and his interest in the estate of WILLIAM McALEXANDER, deceased, and also his interest in all the property now in the possession of his mother, SALLY REYNOLDS, the widow of JOSEPH REYNOLDS; the claim for county land purchased from JEREMIAH BRAMMER; do hereby release and confirm to JAMES REYNOLDS all the above described property, it being the same property conveyed to DeHart in trust for the benefit of Spencer, et als. AARON DeHART, WILLIAM (X) SPENCER, W.J. ROBERTSON, SAMUEL McALEXANDER, PERRY GRAHAM. Witness: WILLIAM AYRES, WILLIAM REYNOLDS, THOMAS DeHART, JAMES REYNOLDS.

Whereas, a suit was instituted in the year 1876 in the name of S. H. CANNADAY against Cannaday's heirs for the purpose of the sale of the lands of WILLIAM CANNADAY, deceased, and whereas Merritt and Baughan were appointed Special Commissioners for that purpose and did sell said lands on August 21, 1876. Whereas, LEWIS BURNETT purchased the lands known as the Clark tract for $307.00. In consideration of the above facts, JOHN MERRITT conveys to LEWIS BURNETT the above lands. March 29, 1878. JOHN MERRITT, Special Commissioner.

Agreement dated September 26, 1888 between WALLER R. STAPLES and JOHN E. PENN. Whereas Staples previously hired Penn as his attorney in a suit pending in the Circuit Court of Patrick County in the name of ISAAC MARTIN'S Executors vs. ABRAM STAPLES Executors in reference to land belonging to ABRAM STAPLES and known as the Anderson Survey, and for such service agreed to give Penn an interest in the proceeds of sale of said land. Whereas ABRAM P. STAPLES, Commissioner of the Circuit Court of Patrick in the case of WALLER R. STAPLES v. PRYER TATUM conveyed to THOMAS B. TATUM 268 acres, which land was sold to satisfy a vendor's lien in favor of WALLER R. STAPLES and whereas JOHN E. PENN assumed to pay to the said Staples for THOMAS B. TATUM the sum of $5.00 per acre for 62-1/4 acres, which has been conveyed to Penn by Tatum and wife. In consideration of the services in said suit and in discharge of the sum, Staples released and discharges Penn from the payment of said sum of $5.00 per acre. WALLER R. STAPLES, JOHN E. PENN. Penn acknowledged in the City of Roanoke and Staples in Montgomery County.

Deed dated January 1, 1883 between WALLER L. HOWARD, Commissioner of the Circuit Court of Floyd County in the cases of J. S. and P. L. HOWARD v. DAVID NOWLIN'S Administrator, et als, JOHN E. MASSEY, Auditor vs. D. & B. NOWLIN and T.B. and D. J. NOWLIN v. JOHN E. MASSEY, Auditor, and J.S. and P.L. HOWARD and T. B. NOWLIN. In pursuance of a decree entered in said cases to partition and allot the lands in the proceeding, and whereas WALLER L. HOWARD was appointed to convey said lands, hereby conveys to T.B. NOWLIN Lot #1 in said report in the Counties of Floyd and Patrick on the waters of Rockcastle Creek, adjoining F. W. EDWARDS.

WALLER L. HOWARD, Commissioner.

Inventory and appraisement of the personal property of MURRY TURNER, a lunatic, September 19, 1887. Total value $340.10. S.H. DUNKLEY, Sheriff. Appraisers: W. B. RUCKER, W.D. VIA, H.M. SCALES. Inventory and appraisement of the personal property of MURRY TURNER, a lunatic, set apart for the use of said lunatic's wife and children and not charged to the Committee. Total - $295.50.

I, BENJAMIN MORRIS, of Henry County, Virginia, have this day sold to GREGORY HAGOOD all my interest in land on Blackberry Creek, and being part of the tract the late THOMAS BAKER died possessed of, adjoining Hagwood, JOHN J. PHILPOTT and STERLING WELLS for the sum of $150.00. March 1, 1843. BENJAMIN MORRIS.

Whereas WILLIAM FLINCHUM, MILTON R. DODSON, and ELIPHAZ SHELTON have purchased from THOMAS BUFORD, attorney in fact for JAMES BUFORD, JR., 688 acres on Russell's Creek at $1.00 per acre to be paid in installments and secured by bonds. July 18, 1836. WILLIAM FLINCHUM, ELIPHAZ SHELTON, MILTON R. DODSON. Witness: CALEB GRIFFITH.

Bill of Sale of property belonging to the estate of GREGORY HAGOOD November 13, 1856 mentions various items of personal property totaling $808.06 and 1 man DAVY purchased by T. J. PENN for $1,075.00, and 1 woman LILLER purchased by J. W. CARTER for $775.00. WILLIAM W. MORRIS, Clerk. J. W. CARTER, Administrator. (Will Book 5, page 174).

HENRY A. WISE, Esquire, Governor of the Commonwealth - Know ye that in conformity with a survey made August 28, 1858 by virtue of Land Office Treasury Warrants Nos. 24.236, 22.830 and 24.684, there is granted to GABRIEL DEAL 140 acres on the headwaters of North Mayo River on the south side of Bull Mountain, adjoining JOSHUA ADAMS. HENRY A. WISE (Deed Book 116, page 267)

Deed dated APRIL 26, 1917 between LETHA BARNARD formerly LETHA HALL and MARTHA VIOLET THOMAS. Consideration of $10.00 conveys her interest in land which she heired by her sister, SARAH ANN HALL'S death, which she died seized and possessed of adjoining CHARLIE NOWLIN and WALTER THOMAS near Charity Church. LETHA BARNARD. Acknowledged before T.S. TERRY, Justice of the Peace. (In an old envelope from LETHA BARNARD, Mayberry, Va. to Mrs. MARTHA VIOLET THOMAS, Buffalo Ridge, Va.)

Deed dated December 12, 1791 in the 15th year of American Independency, between THOMAS ADAMS, Sadler, and ISAAC ADAMS, Planter. Consideration of 100 pounds conveys 428 acres by survey dated April 14, 1780 and being the land granted to THOMAS ADAMS under the hand of THOMAS JEFFERSON, Governor, by patent dated April 10, 1781, and the 5th year of American Independency and also 19 acres adjoining the first tract on the east side and bounded by BRITT STOVALL, it being a tract of 13 acres whereon ISAAC ADAMS now lives. THOMAS ADAMS. Witness: WILLIAM ADAMS, JAMES MARLOW.

Deed dated April 3, 1882 between PLEASANT THOMAS and JAMES THOMAS, his son, gives 200 acres adjoining Franklin County line. PLEASANT THOMAS. Witness: MARTIN CLOUD.

Contract between Dr. E.L. BRANSCOME and T. E. MARSHALL. Consideration of $300.00 paid in advance and 10 bushels of the best winter apples on the farm and all the orchard grass seed that can be saved, the said Marshall is to have 30 acres each year for corn, and he is to put new roller hinges on my new barn at my house and fence off 2 gardens, one on the FRANK SHELOR farm and one on ENOCH COCK'S farm on top of the hill north of ENOCH COCK'S dwelling, and also other maintenance clauses included. April 9, 1912. E. L. BRANSCOME, T. E. MARSHALL. Witness: MARY L. BRANSCOME.

Declaration for Widow's Pension - SUSAN OSBORNE, aged 56 years, appeared and declares that she is the widow of JOHN OSBORNE (record of enlistment and service burned in a house fire); that he died October 7, 1909; that she married under the name of SUSAN ELLIOTT on January 14, 1891 (I had been previously married, but husband was killed while at war.); no children living under the age of 16; P.O. Address is Peter's Creek. SUSAN (X) GOING. A.E. HANDY and W.R. BURGE appeared as witnesses for claimant. September 14, 1916.

June 1, 1909 - Note in the amount of $8.60 given by WILLIAM G. AYERS and EDD AYERS to Virginia-Carolina Chemical Co. for the purchase of fertilizer. WILLIAM G. AYERS, EDD AYERS.

Patrick County - To: C. J. WRIGHT, Surveyor March 23, 1876 - To summonsing hands 3 days $3.00; to W. A. TERRY 3 days plowing single horse and plow 75 cents per day $2.25.
August 20 - To summoning hands 1 day $1.00; to 1 days plowing by WESLEY FOLEY 75 cents; to 1 day for J.J. TERRY 75 cents - Total $2.15. Claim continued.
March, 1877 - 2 days $2.00; 2 days hauling for H.D. WRIGHT with oxen and cart $3.00; 1 day plowing for W. A. TERRY 75 cents; and 1 day plowing for J.J. TERRY 75 cents.

I hereby renounce the provisions in my favor in the Last Will and Testament of my late husband, GABRIEL HYLTON, which was admitted to probate in January, 1875, and elect to take my share in the estate which I may be entitled to under the laws of the Commonwealth. August 16, 1875. LUCY A. HYLTON. Witness: W. CRITZ, JAMES M. SHOCKLEY.

Deed dated October 14, 1885 between JAMES A. PENN and LUCINDA S. PENN, his wife, of Rockingham County, North Carolina to THOMAS PENN of Rockingham County. Consideration of $300.00 conveys 89 acres adjoining SAMUEL P. WILSON, B.H. FLOYD, SUSAN MURPHY and D. H. SHELTON, being the same land conveyed to JAMES PENN from JESSE M. GILES, and known as the old Poindexter lands. Acknowledged in Rockingham County before W. C. STAPLES, Notary Public.

Deed dated July 7, 1877 between RILEY PUCKET and MATILDA PUCKET, his wife, and ELIJAH MARSHALL. Consideration of $10.00 conveys 2 acres on the face of the Blue Ridge on the waters of Lovins Creek. RILEY (X) PUCKET, MATILDA (X) PUCKET. Acknowledged before ROBERT M. CLARK, Notary Public.

Deed dated March 25, 1885 between JAMES S. HARBOUR and Trustees. Conveys a lot 18 feet by 20 feet for church and school purposes so long as it shall be used for such, out of the DICK HALL land directly on the Turnpike where the old Road leaves it, adjoining L.G. RUCKER. JAMES S. HARBOUR.

Cassell, Virginia, June 18, 1907 - Deed between W. G. WAGONER and JENNIE WAGONER, his wife, and Trustees of CHESTNUT RIDGE CHURCH conveys 1 acre on the waters of Grassy Fork of Mayo River, adjoining J. T. GARST. W.G (X) WAGGONER, JENNIE (X) WAGGONER. Witness G. W. GARST.

Deed dated May 5, 1898 between C.R. MARTIN, Clerk of the County Court and A.F. MAYS. Consideration of $1.25, that being the amount of delinquent taxes on lands in the name of Waller & King, containing 38 acres on Elk Creek adjoining LUKE WILLARD, S.H. DUNKLY, W.H. MARTIN, GEORGE W. KING, deceased, and others. C. R. MARTIN.

Deed dated November 15, 1893 between C.E. SMITH and SALLIE E. SMITH, his wife, and P.P. WATSON. Consideration of the exchange of lands and $100.00 conveys Lot No. 15 of the Patrick Springs property and more fully described in a survey by J. H. PEDIGO, Surveyor. C.E. SMITH, SALLIE E. SMITH.

Homestead Deed dated November 8, 1880 by JOHN SHELTON. Whereas, Shelton is a householder and head of a family and desires to avail himself of the homestead act, he hereby declare the following property to be exempt: 20 barrels of corn, 800 pounds of tobacco leaf. JOHN H. SHELTON (X). Witness: CALEB BOYD.

Deed dated May 7, 1881 between THOMAS D. RORER and ARAMINTA RORER, his wife, and FLEMING JAMERSON. Consideration of $300.00 conveys 70 acres on the headwaters of Smith River, adjoining Hylton's old mill pond and JAMES A. INGRAM. T.D. (X) RORRER, ARAMINTA (X) RORER.

Assignment of Territory - I, BOOKER DALTON, did obtain Patent #803.404 for the improvements in plows and cultivators on October 31, 1905 and whereas T. J. GEORGE desires an interest in the same, in consideration of $100.00 assigns all my interest in said invention. March 1, 1910. BOOKER DALTON. Witness: JAMES McHONE, W. C. NOEL.

Deed dated October 3, 1857 between GEORGE Z. EDWARDS and JOSEPH PIKE. Consideration of $400.00 conveys 288 acres according to the patent, on Long Branch on the waters of Peters Creek adjoining GEORGE W. KING, JOSEPH FLIPPEN, BEAN'S KNOB and THOMAS

BEASLEY. (No signatures.)

Deed dated _____, 1876 between C. G. BOWMAN and SUSAN BOWMAN, his wife; JOHN EDWARDS and ARTENSIA EDWARDS, his wife; ALEXANDER EDWARDS and _____ EDWARDS, his wife; and JAMES EDWARDS, heirs and distributees and JOSEPH PIKE. Whereas in 1857 GEORGE Z. EDWARDS sold to Pike 288 acres and did not execute a deed and Pike having paid the $400.00 purchase money is entitled to a deed. And whereas we the heirs of said Edwards being desirous to avoid a suit for title, convey the said 288 acres. (No signatures) Deed prepared for a Surry County, North Carolina notarization.

Deed dated October 24, 1886 between MARSHALL WILLIAMS and DILLIA WILLIAMS, his wife, and S. W. WILLIAMS. Consideration of $50.00 conveys land on the headwaters of Mayo River adjoining JAMES BRANCH. MARSHALL (X) WILLIAMS, DILLA (X) WILLIAMS.

Deed of trust dated May 19, 1881 between J. T. ADAMS, R. J. WOOLWINE, Trustee, to secure a debt of $64.54 to SARAH S. REYNOLDS, Adams conveys in trust 50 acres on the waters of North Mayo River adjoining A. P. ADAMS, MACK FOLEY and others. J.T. ADAMS.

Deed dated October 4, 1893 between J. L. TOMPKINS, surviving Commissioner in the suit of MATTHEW A. MARTIN v. JOSEPH MARTIN and JAMES BRYANT. In pursuance of a decree entered at October Term, 1891, J. L. TOMPKINS and J. T. DOBYNS (died June 21, 1892), did sell at public auction the lands mentioned in said decree and Bryant being the highest bidder of $31.50, said sale being confirmed at June, 1892 term, conveys lands on Smith River formerly belonging to WILLIAM B. MARTIN bounded by JAMES BRYANT, BENJAMIN FOSTER, DANIEL COX, JOHN P. BURRIS and CHARLES BRYANT. J.L. TOMPKINS, Commissioner.

Inventory of goods and wares in the storehouse at Mayo Forge, Virginia, on October 30, 1889 by P.L. PEUER, JR, Trustee, belonging to the firm of E. P. ZENTMEYER & BROS. conveyed to the aforesaid Trustee for the benefit of their creditors. (15 pages of clothing, household and farm items listed for a total value of $1,293.84.

Deed dated June 25, 1870 between SAMUEL G. STAPLES and CAROLINE STAPLES, his wife, and JOSEPH SHELTON. Consideration of $130.00 conveys 13 acres by survey on the waters of South Mayo River. SAMUEL G. STAPLES. (Not notarized)

State of North Carolina, Surry County, July 19, 1879 - I, ELISHA BOWMAN, of Yadkin County, North Carolina appoint M. W. BOWMAN my attorney for me in the Courts of Virginia to (?) 60 acres of land to which I am entitled now in the possession of N.H. GANNDY in the County of (?), Virginia. ELISHA (X) BOWMAN. Acknowledged in Yadkin County before J. W. FLEMING, Justice of the Peace.

Deed of trust dated July 10, 1880 between JERRY STAPLES and JOHN R. NUNN. Staples in order to secure a debt of $13.60 to JOHN E. PENN, conveys in trust his crop of tobacco, corn, fodder and shucks to be raised this year, and all his household furniture. Staples is to clean up the woodland on the east side of the branch near his house on the following terms: Penn is to allow him $3.00 per acre for grubbing the land and to pay him 30 cents a cord for all wood cut. Staples to board himself and furnish his own tools. Work to be done before frost in the fall of 1880. JERRY STAPLES (X).

List of merchandise, accounts, notes and choses in action turned over to P.L. PEURER, JR., Trustee October 30, 1889 by E. P. ZENTMEYER & BROS. for the benefit of their creditors. (Several pages of names listed of people who were indebted for a total of $5,142.01.)

Deed dated Aril 22, 1893 between ANDREW LAWSON and JULINA LAWSON, his wife, and JOHN C. LAWSON and SAMUEL G. ROBERTSON. Consideration of $25.00 and of the grain and all grinding to be done tole free, conveys 1 acre known as the old Handy mill cite on Ivey Creek with the understanding that if the Lawsons are deprived of the above privileges or the mill is let go down and not repaired, the said mill and cite is to go back to the Lawsons. Beginning below the Old Horse Ford . . . . crossing the Old Road . . . . near the head of the Pond, thence down the creek to the BEGINNING. ANDREW (X) LAWSON, JULINA (X) LAWSON, JOHN C. LAWSON.

Homestead Deed dated August 20, 1871 by JOHN CASSELL in pursuance of the homestead act declares the following property exempt: All my interest in the crop now growing on the land of WILLIAM A. BURWELL estimated at $80.00 for 1/4 of the corn crop and garden vegetables, 5 hogs $10.00; 5 sheep $10.00; 3 bee stands $4.50; 2 ploughs and 3 hoes $5.00; 1 cow $15.00; furniture $15.00. JOHN (X) CASSELL.

Agreement dated September 30, 1885 between C.D. LANGHORNE and E.W. BARKSDALE. Whereas Langhorne is the owner of a quantity of valuable walnut lumber growing on what is known as the Newman survey, and desires that the said Barksdale cut the timber. Barksdale agrees to have said timber cut and brought to the depot at Stuart for transportation and Langhorne agrees to pay the cost of cutting and transporting said timber, not to exceed $32.00 per thousand, but it is agreed that Barksdale shall have no control over the sale of said timber or contract any debts for which Langhorne shall be bound. Barksdale is to receive 1/2 of the net proceeds from the sale of said timber after deducting $900.00 advanced by the said Langhorne for the purchase of the timber. C.D. LANGHORNE, E.W. BARKSDALE.

Deed of trust dated April 8, 1887 between J. A. GILBERT and W.B. McCARTHUR, In the consideration of $135.00 to be paid by Gilbert to McCarther, Gilbert puts in trust to T.D. HOWELL 1 pair of mules that lately belonged to G. W. GILBERT, 1 black yoke of cattle; 1 2-horse and 1 4-horse wagon. J.A. GILBERT.

Deed dated March 31, 1886 between WILLIAM McALEXANDER and

SUSANNAH McALEXANDER, his wife, and ANDERSON McALEXANDER. Consideration of $100.00 to be paid in 10 annual installments in labor or any good trade, conveys 75 acres on Rockcastle Creek adjoining GABRIEL DeHART, C.J. DILLON and WILLIAM McGHEE. It is agreed that if the said ANDERSON McALEXANDER shall die without any bodily heirs the land shall revert back to the Grantors or their heirs. WILLIAM McALEXANDER. SUSANAH (X) McALEXANDER.

Agreement dated June 29, 1904 between JAMES A. EANS and C.P. NOLEN. Whereas 141 acres belonging to Eans was sold on January 4, 1904 under a decree of the Circuit Court and was purchased by J.C. DeHART for $804.00. Consideration of $1.00 Eans releases and conveys to Nolen his interest in the proceeds of the sale to Nolen. JAMES A. EANS. Acknowledged before SPARREL WOOD, Justice of the Peace.

Deed of Release dated December 22, 1899 between M. C. GILL, Trustee, JOHNSON GILL & BRO. of Bedford City, Virginia, and W.T. MASSEY, R.H. SHELTON and SUE H. SHELTON. A deed of trust dated July 1, 1897 having been satisfied, the following property is released to Massey and Shelton: 1 18-horsepower locomotive boiler on skids manufactured by A. B. FARQUHAR & CO. and 1 Class 5 engine. M.C. GILL, JOHNSON GILL & BRO.

Homestead Deed dated November 30, 1886 by C.C. CARTER, a householder who avails himself of the homestead exemption, declares the following property: all of his property which was not included in the homestead deed made August 4, 1883, about 300 pounds of tobacco and my crop of corn and wheat. C.C. CARTER.

Whereas in the suit of JAMES G. PENN et als v. GEORGE W. HYLTON et als, P.P. WATSON purchased Lot 55 and W.C. McLANE purchased No. 66, which sales were confirmed about May 29, 1891, and the parties have made an equal exchange of said lands. This deed made November 15, 1893 between P.P. WATSON and ADDIE M. WATSON, his wife, and W.C. McLEAN and ELLA P. McLEAN, his wife, in consideration of an exchange of lands, this deed is to be taken as authorizing said P. BOULDIN, JR., Commissioner to convey title to the said property. P.P. WATSON, ADDIE M. WATSON, W.C. McLEAN, E.P. McLEAN. Watson acknowledged in Henry County and McLeans in Guilford County, North Carolina.

Deed dated February 18, 1889 between T.D. RORRER and ARMINDA RORRER, his wife, MARSHALL WILLIAMS and DILLAMANDA WILLIAMS, his wife, and SAMUEL WILLIAMS and ELIZABETH WILLIAMS, his wife, and ISAAC JONES. Consideration of $510.00 conveys 5 acres on South Mayo, it being the mill property on said Turnpike sold by T.D. RORRER to said Williams and sons, but no deed having been made, and he having sold the said property to Jones, all parties join in this deed. T.D. (X) RORRER, MARSHALL (X) WILLIAMS. (Not notarized)

Deed dated April 25, 1901 between G.B. GUNTER and LUCY G. GUNTER, his wife, AND J.C. GUNTER. Consideration of $20.00 conveys 20 acres on Dan River, it being part of G. B. GUNTER tract deeded to him by JOHN HOOKER and wife. G.B. GUNTER, L.G. GUNTER.

Consideration of $75.00 we do grant to Patrick County the privilege of using the patent known as the Campbell Patent Index for deeds free from all other royalty bonuses. E.A. CAMPBELL by W.R. WOOLWINE, his attorney in fact. May 13, 1881.

Deed dated April 29, 1889 between JAMES S. HARBOUR and School Trustees of Mayo River School District. Consideration of $15.00 conveys 1/2 acre adjoining JOHN BURWELL. JAMES S. HARBOUR.

Deed dated July 19, 1884 between JOHN T. CARTER and SARAH H. CARTER, his wife, and LUCINDA R. BOYD of Floyd County. Consideration of $100.00 conveys 55-1/4 acres on Rockcastle Creek adjoining JOSEPH CARTER, BENJAMIN BELCHER, deceased. JOHN T. CARTER. SARAH H. CARTER.

Last Will and Testament of PHILLIP PENN - All just debts to be paid. To my sons, GEORGE PENN, WILSON PENN and GABRIEL PENN each 1 shilling; to my daughters, FANNY FULCHER, LUCY HANNA, MILLY ROSS, SCINTHA SNEED and NANCY TAYLOR each 1 shilling; to my daughter, SALLY NORTON, 40 pounds; to my son, ABRAHAM PENN, 1 negro boy named WASHINGTON, 1 horse saddle and bridle which is now in his possession, 1 feather bed and furniture and 210 acres of land to be laid off on the upper part whereon I now live; to my daughter PATSEY PENN 1 negro woman named AIMEY, 1 feather bed and furniture; to my grandsons, PHILLIP PENN and EDMUND PENN 150 acres of land on the lower part of my tract adjoining lands devised to my son, Abraham. All the residue of my estate to be divided between Wilson, Abraham and Patsey. Should my son Abraham incline to sell his land before my 2 grandsons arrive at age 21, then my Executors are authorized to sell their part or at the time they deem it advisable to sell, they are authorized to use their discretion and the money to be put upon interest until they arrive at full age. My part of the land in Kentucky which I succeeded by the death of my brother, William, to be sold for the benefit of my children, Wilson, Abraham and Patsey. Executors my son WILSON PENN and my nephew, GEORGE PENN. November 29, 1802. PHILIP PENN. Witness: JOSEPH STOVALL, GREENVILLE PENN, SALLEY PENN, ABRAHAM (X) GOSSETT, JOHN (X) MEDLEY, SR. Proved July, 1806.

Know all men by these presents that I, ELIZABETH L. STUART, appoint SAMUEL G. STAPLES my attorney in fact to sign my name and deliver as security any bond which the County Court of Patrick may require of my son, W. ALEXANDER STUART, on appointing him the personal representative of his father, ARCHIBALD STUART, deceased. March 24, 1856. ELIZABETH L. STUART.

Deed dated December 22, 1884 between O.H. SHELTON and MARY E. SHELTON, his wife, and GEORGE W. CLARK, GEORGE GILBERT and WILLIAM CRITZ, Trustees of Mayo School District. Consideration of $15.00 conveys 1 acre on the waters of Mill Creek. O.H. SHELTON, MARY E. SHELTON. Acknowledged before JOSEPH H. CLARK, Justice of the Peace.

I hereby nominate JOSIAH FERRIS of Nashville, Tennessee, my attorney in fact to collet any money which may be due my wife, MOLLIE H. FERRIS, formerly MOLLIE H. PENN, either in Tennessee or from T. J. PENN of Patrick County, who is administrator or executor of CLARK PENN, deceased, from her late father's estate. April 1, 1867. THOMAS B. FERRIS. Acknowledged in New Orleans, Louisiana before ANDREW HEW, JR., Notary Public.

Deed of Gift from GEORGE R. FULCHER to RUTH E. FULCHER. In consideration of the love and affection I have for my wife and children, LUCY E. FULCHER, MARTHA A. FULCHER, NANCY E. FULCHER, MARY A. FULCHER, SUSAN FULCHER, or any other children I may have at my death, conveys 2 milk cows, 9 hogs, 4 sheep, 2 bee stands, 1 oxen, 2 bedsteads and bedding, 1 safe and its contents, 1 chest, 1 clock, cooking utensils, and all other household property I possess, 1 set of mechanic tools. September 15, 1873. G.R. FULCHER.

Deed dated January 13, 1905 between WALTER P. CLARK and BOB REYNOLDS, IDA REYNOLDS, GEORGE REYNOLDS, and RICHARD PENN. Consideration of $198.00 conveys 36 acres on Mill Creek. WALTER P. CLARK. Acknowledged before G.W. HARRIS, Justice of the Peace.

Deed dated March 15, 1878, between RICHARD PICKERAL, a householder and head of a family and desiring to entitle himself to the homestead exemption, declare the following property: 1 red heifer about 2 years old, 1 black heifer 1 year old, 3 bee stands, bedding, 1 bureau, 1/2 of 1,000 pounds of leaf tobacco. RICHARD (X) PICKERAL.

Deed dated March 2, 1906 between M.V. STEDMAN and SALLIE STEDMAN, his wife, and GEORGE F. SMART. Consideration of $266.68 conveys 20 acres on Big Ivey Creek. M.V. STEDMAN, SALLIE W. STEDMAN, G.F. SMART.

Agreement (no date) between JAMES STAPLES and JAMES RUCKER. Staples leases to Rucker all that part of the bottom east of Campbell Mill Creek, and right of the Turnpike, to the lane leading from the Turnpike to the ford below the quarter down to a sink or drain in said bottom, including the house where Gabr. Penn now lives, commencing on January 1 next and ending December 31, 1874. Staples to split enough rails to do the fence good from the mill creek along the Turnpike to the land and along the land to the creek at the water gap, and to assist in putting said rails on the fence. Rucker is to break with a 2-horse plow said Staples part of the bottom and to lay off same for planting in corn and to plow the corn 2 times and to haul the rails for said fence. JAMES (X) STAPLES, JAMES (X) RUCKER.

Copy of will of ROBERT BRADY of Carroll County, Virginia. To son THOMAS BRADY all my personal property and 33 acres and 44 poles of land, 22-1/2 acres known as the Radford land and 10 acres and 124 poles known as the WILL HENDRIX land; daughter JULIA J. BRADY 10 acres part of 40 acre tract; daughter PENINA BRADY 10 acres part of a 40 acre tract, daughter ISABELLA A. BRADY 10 acres part of a 40 acre tract; youngest son JAMES A. BRADY 10 acres last of said 40 acre tract; daughter, MARY E. SINCEBOUTH $1.00; daughter LETHA A. AYERS $1.00; 2 heirs of my daughter RACHEL PARTUS, deceased $1.00 each; son ROBERT A. BRADY $1.00. Executor J.H. MARSHALL. Dated October 2, 1914. (X) ROBERT BRADY. Witnesses: E.A. MARTIN, M.M. FARISS. Probated October 12, 1917 in Carroll County.

Suit was filed to partition the lands of which DELILIA BRADY and ROBERT BRADY died seized and possessed. J.E. BOWMAN, J.W. KINZER, MONROE FARISS, ARTHUR MARTIN and CLERIN MARTIN were appointed Commissioners to partition lands and did so as follows: PENINA BRADY Lot #1 - 19=57/100 acres; Lot #2 JAMES A. BRADY - 20 acres; Lot #3 ISABELLA A. BRADY - 21-56/100 acres; Lot #4 JULIA J. BRADY - 26-1/2 acres; Lot #5 THOMAS BRADY - 18-10/100 acres; Lot #6 ROBERT A. BRADY - 18-06/1-- acres; and Lot #7 ALITHA ANN AYRES - 20-38/100 acres.

Hillsville, Virginia - March 4, 1856 - Mr. JACKSON VIA; Sir, I have seen the office that Mr. Hale put your debt in the hands of. He says that he has taken judgment against JOHN HANDY for you, but thinks he cannot make anything out of him. I have tried to shave off the debt, but cannot sell it. Therefore, I return you the officer receipt. Yrs Respty EDWARD COCKRAM by F.L. HALE. To: WILLIAM R. RADFORD, Long Branch P.O., Franklin County, Virginia.

Twelve months after date with interest I promise to pay to J. S. MARTIN $95.00 for 2 acres of land. April 8, 1918. JAMES MILLS. Witness: B.F. OVERBY. Paid in full February 24, 1919.

Deed dated January 5, 1909, between BETTY DEAL and J.H. STOVALL. In consideration that Stovall binds himself firmly to keep well fenced and furnish pasture to Deal so long as she lives on the place where she now lives for 2 head of cattle and 2 sheep, conveys all her interest in 7 acres on the headwaters of North Mayo River adjoining JOHN H. ADAMS and J.H. STOVALL. BETTY (X) DEAL. Witness: G.W. HARRIS .

Deed dated May 27, 1901 between GEORGE D. HUBBARD and A.H. STAPLES. By a decree of Court entered October term, 1896, in the cause of J.L O'MARA et als vs. M.W. WEDDLE et als, Hubbard was appointed Special Commissioner to sell at public auction the DANIEL O'MARA homeplace thought to contain 90 acres, but since ascertained to be 82 acres adjoining PETER BELCHER, J.D. CRUISE, E.J. HYLTON, mountain road leading up Smith River Gap, and at said sale Staples made the highest bid of $525.00 and became the purchaser thereof. GEORGE D. HUBBARD, Special Commissioner.

Deed dated September 3, 1915 between NANCY J. STOOPS and J.W. AYERS. Consideration of $292.50 conveys 19-1/2 acres on the waters of South Mayo River adjoining J.T. CARTER, W.I. CRADDOCK. (No signatures)

Deed dated March 28, 1912 between A.S. MARTIN and MAGGIE L. MARTIN, his wife, and J.S. FULCHER, Trustee, conveys in trust to secure $82.40 due to R.W. MORRISON for 31 acres on waters of North Mayo River and bounded by A.W. MARTIN. A.S. MARTIN, MAGGIE L. MARTIN. (Paid October 22, 1912)

Deed dated January 14, 1913 between M.E. STAPLES, W.P. STAPLES, T.M. STAPLES, CARRIE STAPLES, L.J. STAPLES and LELIA H. SHOCKLEY to A.H. STAPLES. Consideration of $300.00 conveys all their right, title and interest in 30 acres on the waters of the south fork of South Mayo River adjoining FLORA A. STAPLES, JUSTIN McINTOSH, W.H. RICKMAN and MARY E. STAPLES. L.J. STAPLES, CARRIE S. TURNER.

Deed dated May 14, 1883 between ASA WOOD and JANE WOOD, his wife, and W.H. ANGLIN and LEOTA ANGLIN, his wife to WILLIAM L. FULCHER. Consideration of $300.00 conveys 92 acres on Matthews Creek. ASA WOOD, JANE (X) WOOD, LEOTA ANGLIN, W.H. ANGLIN.

Deed dated March 25, 1902, between SAMUEL W. WILLIAMS and W.F. WRIGHT. Consideration of $200.00 conveys 102 acres by survey, known as the WILSON HAIRSTON place on the waters of the Bull Mountain fork of South Mayo River. S.W. WILLIAMS .

Deed dated April 29, 1901 between JOHN ADKINS and NANNIE A. ADKINS, his wife, and WALTER F. WRIGHT. Consideration of $25.00 conveys 8-1/2 acres on South Mayo River. JOHN ADKINS, NANNIE A. ADKINS.

Deed dated April 29, 1901 between JOHN ADKINS and NANNIE A. ADKINS, his wife, and ENOS HYLTON and MATTIE J. HYLTON, his wife, to WALTER F. WRIGHT. Consideration of $186.96 conveys 60 acres on South Mayo River. JOHN ADKINS, NANNIE A. ADKINS, ENOS HYLTON, MATTIE J. HYLTON.

Deed dated September 2, 1899 between D.W. SCOTT and SUSAN M. SCOTT, his wife, and DANIEL S. SCOTT and MARY A. SCOTT, his wife, to B.R. PENDLETON. Consideration of $1,050.00 conveys 65 acres and 20-1/2 acres on Ivey Creek adjoining JOHN W. SCOTT, J.A. WOOD, and the second tract being the same land D.W. SCOTT purchased from LUCY SCOTT and N.B. SCOTT. D.W. SCOTT, S.M. SCOTT, DANIEL S. SCOTT, MARY A. (X) SCOTT. (Deed Book 33, page 465)

Deed dated April 11, 1911 between WALTER GOINS and MARY GOINS to WALTER CULLER. Consideration of $30.00 conveys 3 acres on Clark's Creek adjoining WALTER CULLER and MILLARD CULLER. WALTER (X) GOINS, MARY M. GOINS. Witness: W.E. CRAWFORD.

Deed dated October 17, 1891 between JOHN SALMONS, SR. and SARAH SALMONS, his wife; MARK SALMONS and SARAH SALMONS, his wife; DAVID G. SALMONS and AMANDA J. SALMONS to MARTHA COCKRAM. Whereas, by the will of JESSE JONES he devised to JOHN SALMONS and SARAH SALMONS land on Widgeon Creek for their lives and at their deaths to their heirs; and whereas all parties have mutually divided the lands among the heirs of said JOHN SALMONS and SARAH SALMONS. Consideration of the premises and $1.00 conveys 33 acres adjoining

DAVID J. SALMONS, P. McALEXANDER. JOHN (X) SALMONS, SARAH (X) SALMONS, MARK SALMONS, SARAH (X) SALMONS, DAVID G. SALMONS, AMANDA J. (X) SALMONS.

Deed dated May 31, 1919 between R.E. WRIGHT to A.D. MARTIN. Consideration of $5.00 conveys 1/15 of an acre on the waters of Smith River. R.E. WRIGHT.

Deed dated February 28, 1894 between DAVID W. ARMSTRONG, Widower, of New York to SIDNEY D. FRESHMAN of same. Consideration of $1.00 conveys the following lands in Patrick and Henry Counties, (1) that tract granted by the State of Virginia to WILLIAM BRECKENRIDGE and WILLIAM BOWYER by patent dated July 5, 1796, containing 35,000 acres adjoining JOSEPH GALLEGOE on Goblingtown Creek, Blackberry Creek, Bowings Creek and Smith River; (2) patent to Breckenridge and Bowyer dated July 5, 1796 containing 65,000 acres adjoining JOHN MILLER on Dan River, Buzzard Branch, Ararat River, and JOHN CREED. DAVID W. ARMSTRONG.

Deed dated August 3, 1908 between FANNIE NOWLIN to ESSIE M. PHILLIPS. Consideration of the love and affection, and that Phillips will comfortably maintain and support Nowlin for her natural life and pay all her doctor's bills which may accrue by reason of her infirmities and also to support her brother, ARCH S. NOWLIN, during the remainder of his life and if said Phillips shall have no children living at her death, the land to revert to Nowlin's estate, conveys 2 acres in the Town of Stuart known as MAT SMITH land, being a part of the land conveyed to Nowlin from MAT SMITH, adjoining Clark and Depot Street and South Main Street. FANNIE NOWLIN.

Deed dated August 1, 1910 between FRANK BEASLEY and LUCY BEASLEY to GEORGE R. BEASLEY. Consideration of $50.00 conveys 1/8 interest in 81 acres on the waters of Peters Creek (less 20 acres cut off), being the land deeded to FRANK BEASLEY by R.M. BEASLEY et als. FRANK (X) BEASLEY, LUCY (X) BEASLEY. Witness to Marks: W.C. LESTER.

Deed dated June 11, 1898 between ADELINE HANDY, widow of S.A. HANDY, to S.E. HANDY. Whereas, S.A. HANDY in his lifetime sold to S.E. HANDY 100 acres, and died before a deed could be made and all purchase money having been paid, conveys all her right, title and interest in said land. ADELINE HANDY (X).

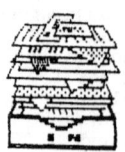

INDEX

ABBINGTON - 1

ABRAM - 25,54

ADAMS - 11,12,16,19,20,26,29,39, 52,53,56,57,59

ADKIN(S) - 39,65

AFRICAN METHODIST EPISCOPAL CHURCH - 16

AGEE - 2

AIMEY - 62

AKERS\ACRES - 12,15,16,24,29, 30,35,39,48

ALDERMAN - 43

ALEXANDER - 9,53

ALLEN - 12,33,34,41,42

ALVIS - 53

AMERICA - 25

ANDERSON - 21,44

ANGLIN - 44,65

ANTHONY - 25

ARMSTRONG - 34,50,66

ARNOLD - 13,14,26,28,39

ARON - 25

ARRINGTON - 30

ASHWORTH - 43

ASKEW - 14,38

AUSTIN - 12,25

AYERS - 1,4,5,8,9,10,12,19, 29,31,37,39,51,53,55,57,64

BAKER - 19,56

BALDWIN - 23,30

BALISLE - 27,35,45,46,54

BANKS - 5,11,27

BARLEY - 9

BARKER - 18

BARKSDALE - 23,60

BARNARD - 13,25,33,50,56

BARNET - 25

BARROTT\BARRETT - 4,21

BARTLETT - 36

BARTON - 43

BAYLOR - 13

BEAMER - 42

BEAN'S KNOB - 58

BEASLEY - 14,25,45,59,66

BELCHER - 31,53,62,64

BELL - 20,50

BILL - 11

BINGHAM\BINGMAN - 18,26,27,35

BISHOP - 17,38,40,44,45

BLACKARD - 6,23

1

BLACKBURN - 16

BLANCET - 25

BOILES\BOYLES - 11,18,36

BOLING\BOWLING\BOULDIN - 27,28,
32,41,45,61

BOLT - 9

BOOKER - 3

BOOTH - 9

BOWMAN - 20,21,25,37,59,64

BOWYER - 66

BOYD - 14,19,25,26,44,52,53,
55,58

BRADY - 63,64

BRAGEN - 12

BRAMMER - 38,16,18,30,53,55

BRANCH - 59

BRANHAM - 11

BRANSCOME - 57

BRANSON - 9,53

BREAM - 25

BRECKENRIDGE - 66

BRISTOW - 17

BROWN - 8,14,21,41,47,49,50,53

BRYANT - 24,35,59

BUFORD - 34,41,56

BURGE - 18,24,36,50,57

BURNETT - 8,11,16,17,27,33,
35,40,47,54,55

BURRIS - 50,59

BURWELL - 5,38,42,54,60,62

BUZZARD - 14,46

CALLOWAY - 1,11

CAMPBELL - 5,6,37,38,49,62

CANADAY\CANNADAY - 9,55

CANNON - 15,26

CAREY - 48

CARROLL - 33

CARTER - 2,5,6,8,9,11,12,
16,25,28,29,32,35,45,52,
56,61,62,64

CASSELL\CASTLE - 5,10,21,
45,53,60

CATHERINE - 25

CAYWOOD - 30

CHAMBERS - 13,23,30,34,43

CHANDLER - 45

CHANEY - 45

CHAVERS - 39

CHEATHAM - 21,33

CHERRY - 26,28,34

CHESTNUT RIDGE CHURCH - 58

CHILDRESS - 7

CLANTON - 22

<u>2</u>

CLARK\CLARKE - 1,6,7,8,10,14,
18,19,20,24,26,28,35,37,42,
47,49,51,58,62,63

CLAY - 1,31

CLEMENT - 33

CLOSE - 11

CLOUD - 8,9,10,19,28,47,
49,57

COCK - 33,50,57

COCKRAM - 12,51,64,65

COLEMAN\COLDMOND - 52

COLLINS\COLLINGS - 4,15,18,24,
25,36,50

COMBS - 34

CONCIL - 37

CONNER - 4,12,16,37,44,53

CONYWAY - 6

COOK - 50,51

CORN - 12,33,39,42,46,49,50

COSS - 29

COX - 17,19,35,39,59

CRADDOCK - 3,7,14,15,16,39,64

CRAVEN - 31

CRAWFORD - 27,43,65

CREED - 47,54

CRITZ - 3,5,8,9,11,18,25,29,
44,46,47,52,54,57,62

CROWDER - 19

CRUISE - 52,54,64

CRUMP - 15

CULLER - 65

CURATHO - 53

DALTON - 6,30,41,49,58

DAN RIVER DISTRICT OF
PUBLIC SCHOOLS - 13

DANIEL - 34,43

DAVID - 54

DAVIS - 3,12,53

DAVY - 56

DAWSON - 9,44

DEAN - 10

DEARMAN - 8

DEATHERIDGE - 29

DEHART\DEHEART - 3,6,9,12,
13,16,17,19,26,28,34,36,40,
43,48,49,53,54,55,60

DESHAZO - 48

DEWEZE - 11

DICKERSON - 25

DICKINSON - 53

DILLARD - 37

DILLON\DILLION - 4,5,14,19,
34,39,41,44,52,53,60

DISE - 56,64

DOBYNS - 44,59

DODSON\DOTSON - 1,2,4,11,12,
17,19,36,53,56

DOUGLAS - 31

DUFFIELD - 27

DUNCAN - 25,53

DUNKLEY - 56,58

DURHAM - 4,14,25

DUVALL - 19

EANS - 51,60

EARLS -39,53

EARLY - 33

EAST - 15,19

EATON - 49

EDWARDS - 4,7,12,17,52,55,
58,59

ELGIN\ELGAN - 17,54

ELKINS - 18

ELLIOTT - 19,57

ELLIS - 7

EMILY - 25

ENNIS - 20

EPPERSON - 10,25,38

FAIN - 4,5,6,8,15,21,45,54

FARIS\FARISS - 54,64

FARQUHAR - 61

FERGERSON - 28,35

FERRIS - 11,63

FIELDS - 36

FISHER - 16

FITZGERALD - 23,24,49

FLEMING - 47,59

FLETCHER - 7,29

FLINCHUM - 56

FLIPPEN - 33,58

FLOWERS - 12

FLOYD - 2,25,26,57

FOLEY - 10,11,13,24,28,46,
50,57,59

FORKNER - 19

FOSTER - 3,4,10,19,26,27,
37,40,59,62

FOWLKES - 49

FRANCE\FRANS - 1,7,18,34

FRANCIS - 3

FRASHURE\FRAZURE - 23

FRENCH - 11

FRESHMAN - 66

FULCHER - 2,3,63,65

GADDIS - 30

GALLANT - 15

GARLAND - 50

GARST - 58

GARVEN - 54

GEORGE - 31,58

GILBERT - 5,10,12,14,15,23,
24,60,62

GILES - 57

GILL - 60

GILMER - 50

GODARD - 39

GOINS\GOING\GOWING\GOWIN - 7,
13,16,19,28,30,37,48,57,65

GOODE - 12

GOSSETT - 66

GRADY - 53

GRAHAM - 15,25,54,55

GRAVELY - 51

GRAVES - 6

GRAY - 8,14,31,54

GRAYBEEL - 35

GREEN - 54

GREENWOOD - 4,15,47,49

GREGG\GRIGG - 19,34,52

GRIFFITH - 46,54,56

GRIMES - 15

GROVE - 30

GUNTER - 15,51,61,62

GUYNN - 37

HAGOOD - 56

HAIRSTON - 8,11,12,15,16,
28,35,38,39,44,47,49,50,
65

HALE - 46,53,64

HALEY - 16

HALL - 1,5,9,12,14,15,20,
27,28,30,36,48,50,52,56

HAMER - 9

HAMMITT - 13,23,30,31

HANBY - 9,17,33,35,45

HANCOCK - 35,40

HANDY - 6,14,29,57,64,66

HANKS - 6

HARBOUR - 2,27,28,37,40,45,
58,62

HARMAN - 31

HARRIS - 15,18,19,21,22,25,
27,29,41,48,49,52,54,63,64

HATCHER - 6,25,26,36,42,53

HAYNES\HANES - 5,11,20,28,
34,35,62

HEATH - 39

HEFFLEFINGER - 54

HELMS - 41

HENDERSON - 50

HENRY - 25,50

HENSDALE - 37

HENSLEY - 25

HENSON - 15

HEW - 63

HIATT - 6,10,35,36

HICKENGBOTTOM - 48

HICKS\HIX - 39,52

HILL - 11,14,29,39

HINES - 6,34,51

HOGE - 21,42

HOLLANDSWORTH - 2,19

HOOKER - 14,29,30,41,45,62

HOPKINS - 28,42

HOPPER - 7

HORD - 15

HOUNCHELL - 33

HOUCHINS - 16,19,27,45,53

HOWARD - 8,55,56

HOWELL - 4,7,14,15,16,17,23, 28,35,40,43,45,53,54

HUBBARD - 3,31,36,39,53,64

HUDNALL - 8

HUDSON - 12

HUGHES - 15,16,25,46,48,49

HUNT - 17

HURD\HERD\HEARD - 7,26,40,42

HURT - 12,35

HUTCHENS - 44

HYLTON - 11,18,22,29,31,32, 47,51,53,57,61,64,65

INGRAM\INGRUM - 2,16,17,54, 58

INSCORE - 24

ISOM - 18

JAMERSON - 30,58

JAMES - 44

JANEY - 41

JEFFERSON - 21,22,56

JOHNSON - 10,16,32,33

JONES - 5,15,26,27,46,61

JOYCE - 7,15,16,18,36,38, 39,42,44,53

JUNE - 25

KAMMERER - 13,39,40

KASEY - 34,36

KEATON - 2,3,19,36,51,54

KELLAR - 8

KELLY - 28, 29,39

KENDRICK - 12

KENNERLY - 1,36,44

KINCANNON - 50

KING - 9,22,25,36,38,43, 45,53,58

KIRK - 30

KOGER - 1,14,40,53

LACKEY - 28,49

<u>6</u>

LANE - 33

LANGHORNE - 60

LANMUM - 9

LAURENCE - 10,53

LAW - 6,13

LAWLESS - 20,54

LAWSON - 32,34,47,50,60

LAYMAN - 16,21

LEAKE - 11

LEE - 11,16,29,34,36,39,53

LEMONS - 26

LESTER - 31,32,66

LEWIS - 7,12,13,25,30,39,54

LIGHT - 32,42,53,54

LILLER - 56

LITCHENS - 47

LITTRALE - 29

LIZZIE - 1

LOWE - 20

LUCY -25,28

LYBROOK - 18,19,20,23,26,29

LYON - 9,10,53

MABE - 40

MANKINS - 13

MANNIN - 46

MARKLE - 27

MARLOW - 57

MARSH - 6

MARSHALL - 1,12,24,35,52, 57,58,64

MARTHA - 25

MARTIN - 2,5,6,7,8,11,13, 14,16,18,20,24,26,29,30, 37,38,39,40,45,46,50,51, 54,55,58,59,64,65,66

MARTINDALE - 36

MASSEY - 12,35,36,55,61

MATTHEWS - 1,9,44

MAY(S) - 2,8,58

MAYO - 27

MCALEXANDER - 27,44,50,54, 55,60,61,65

MCCABE - 1

MCCANLESS - 19,38

MCCARTHUR - 60

MCCRAW - 8,25,45,48

MCDONALD - 34

MCGEE\MEGEHEE - 47,53,61

MCGOWN\MCGOWAN - 26,53

MCGRIFFIN - 37

MCHONE - 58

MCINTOSH - 65

MCKENZIE - 28

7

MCLANE - 61

MCLEN\MCLEAN - 21,61

MCMILLIAN - 1,9,14,20,23,37,38

MCPEAK - 44,54

MEADOWS - 13

MEDLEY - 62

MENDENHALL - 24

MEREDITH - 45,53

MERRITT - 44,55

METCALF - 45

METHODIST EPISCOPAL CHURCH - 1

METHVIN - 11

MIDDLETON - 34

MIDKIFF - 44

MILLER - 20,21,47

MILLS - 46,64

MILLY - 25

MITCHELL - 2,13,23,31,38,51

MIZE - 16

MOIR - 15,21,26,27,40

MOIR, SPENCER & BROWN - 42

MONDAY - 48

MONFORD - 23

MONTGOMERY - 23,24

MOORE\MOOR - 4,6,9,18,25,30, 33,38,44,47

MORAN - 53

MOREFIELD - 25

MORRIS - 5,18,35,56

MORRISON\MORISON - 25,54,65

MOSER - 7

MOSS - 27

MOUNT PLEANSANT CHURCH - 1

MULLINS - 37

MURPHY - 11,29,36,39,40,48, 52,57

MURROW - 1

MURRY - 35

MYERS - 5

NANCY - 54

NEWMAN\NUMAN - 17,19,23,47

NICHOLS - 32

NOAH - 27

NOE - 19

NOEL - 8,16,31,48,49,58

NOLEN - 42,43,51,60

NORTON - 62

NOWLIN - 3,8,15,17,19,23, 27,30,55,56,66

NUNN - 54,59

OBRYAN - 36

OMARA - 64

OSBORNE - 30,57

OSCAR - 25

OVERBY - 6,27,64

OVERSTREET - 22

PACK - 19

PADGETT - 8

PALMER - 34

PANNILL\PANNEL - 5,11,22,29,44

PARKER - 2,12,35

PARR - 6,7,52

PARSONS - 48

PATTERSON - 4

PAYNE - 8

PEATROSS - 15

PEDIGO - 19,20,32,51,58

PENDLETON - 65

PENN - 1,3,8,9,16,19,21,26, 32,34,36,38,39,41,43,44,46, 47,50,51,52,55,56,57,59,61, 62,63

PERKINS - 38,44,55

PERROW - 23

PETER - 25

PEUER - 59,60

PHILIS - 25

PHILLIPS - 10,66

PHILPOTT - 4,19,21,56

PICKEREL - 26,53,63

PIKE - 58,59

PINKARD - 23

PLASTERS - 35,38,49

POLLARD - 47

POOR\POORE - 29,45

PORTUS\PARTUS - 24,64

POSEY - 39

POTTER - 41

PRESTON - 29

PRICE - 1,12,46,49,54

PRILLAMAN\PRILEAMAN - 10, 19,49

PROPHET - 16,44

PRUNTY - 1

PUCKET - 9,32,35,58

PURDY - 4,22

QUARLES - 53

QUIXOTE - 25

RADFORD - 64

RAKES - 14,22,33,37

RANDOLPH - 11

RANGELEY - 8,19,27,31,32, 38,47

RATLIFF - 6,12,29

REA - 26

REDD - 11,21,23,39,51

REED - 22,33,40

REEVES - 19

REYNOLDS - 9,11,17,18,19,26,
36,42,45,46,53,54,55,59,63

RICKMAN - 10,65

ROBERSON - 17,26,37

ROBERTS - 39

ROBERTSON\ROBINSON - 2,6,17,22,
27,32,49,52,54,55,60

RODOLPHUS - 25

ROGERS - 6,20,33,48,49,53

RORRER - 13,20,21,28,44,54,
58,61

ROSENBAUM - 40

ROSS - 27,40,43,51,62

ROWAN & SCOTT - 5

RUBLE - 43

RUCK - 52

RUCKER - 1,3,7,20,24,27,31,32,
33,34,36,40,42,43,44,48,50,56,
58,63

RUFFIN - 23

RUSSELL - 34

RYAN - 27

SALMONS - 52,65,66

SANDLIN - 6

SANDEFUR - 14

SAUNDERS - 27

SCALES - 1,4,5,38,44,46,
47,56

SCHOOL TRUSTEES OF SMITH
RIVER DISTRICT - 29

SCOTT - 10,25,50,65

SHARP - 17,50,53

SHELOR\SHEYLOR - 12,13,21,
28,31,37,44,57

SHELTON - 1,2,3,5,6,11,17,
19,20,21,22,23,25,27,28,29,
38,39,47,51,56,57,58,59,61,
62

SHOCKLEY - 41,57,65

SHORT - 16,27,36

SHOUGH - 51

SIMMONS - 29

SIMS - 31,49

SINCEBOUTH - 64

SIZEMORE - 35

SKOAN - 42

SLAYDON - 51

SLON\SLONE - 18

SLUSHER - 47

SMALLMAN - 39

SMART - 6,36,63

SMITH - 1,3,6,7,10,11,13,
18,19,20,24,25,26,31,32,
33,35,37,52,58,66

SNEED - 12,19,62

SNOW - 5,9
SNYDER - 13
SOUDER - 45
SOUTHERN - 19
SOWERS - 39
SPARGER - 45
SPENCER - 4,6,23,34,50,51,54,55
STANLEY - 12,24,33,39,47
STAPLES - 2,3,4,6,8,10,11,16,19,20,21,23,24,25,31,32,33,37,39,41,42,48,49,50,51,55,57,59,60,62,63,64
STEADMAN - 20,26,63
STEPHENS - 2,46
STIGGLER - 16
STOARD - 3,4
STONE - 31
STOOPS - 64
STOVALL - 2,5,12,34,37,50,56,64,65
STRONG - 5
STUART - 8,62
STUMBLE - 25
SUTHERLAND - 43

TALBOT - 34,35
TALLEY - 31
TAMSEY - 54

TATE - 1
TATUM - 3,11,18,26,29,41,55
TAYLOR - 2,5,9,10,11,15,17,20,30,31,32,34,39,41,45,46,53,62
TENISEN\TENISON - 3,33
TERRY - 7,56,57
THOMAS - 1,13,17,26,33,56,57
THOMPSON - 25,30,38
THURMOND - 4
TILLEY - 4,14,15
TINNEY - 2,29
TITTLE - 43,53
TOLBERT - 43
TOMPKINS - 59
TOWNLEY - 28,32
TREDWAY - 16
TRENT - 34,39,41
TRUMTOWER - 40
TUDER\TUDOR - 28,46
TUGGLE - 3,6,23,24,28,29,31,38,52,53,54
TURNER - 2,6,9,12,17,20,24,30,32,33,40,41,44,46,49,51,56,65

UNDERWOOD - 53
UNTHANK - 37

VARNER - 36

VASS - 14

VAUGHAN\VAUGHN - 17,25,45

VAWTER - 48

VEST - 1,7

VIA - 1,12,17,22,35,37,45,56,64

VIPPERMAN - 53

WADE - 52

WAGONER - 58

WALDEN - 15,16

WALKER - 44

WALLER - 44,48

WALTER(S) - 34,35,48

WARE - 35

WARRICK - 45

WASHINGTON - 53,62

WATKINS - 25,49

WATSON - 50,58,61

WATTS - 38

WAUHOP - 21,33

WEAVER - 49

WEBB - 33,39,41,50,54

WEDDLE - 64

WEST - 2,12,14,19,23,38

WHITE - 48

WHITLOCK - 41

WHITTLE - 44

WIATT - 34

WIGFALL - 30,43

WIGGINGTON - 10,40

WILLARD - 52,58

WILLIAMS - 4,15,27,34,39,
40,41,45,59,61,65

WILLIS - 1,48

WILLS - 23,50,56

WILSON - 33,57

WIMBISH - 24,36,47

WISE - 56

WISLER - 20

WITT - 15,19,20,27,45,50

WONDERLAND - 48

WOOD\WOODS - 10,12,20,32,
33,34,36,43,52,60,65

WOOLWINE - 5,20,31,38,41,
59,62

WRIGHT - 24,32,57,65,66

YEATTS - 23

YOUNG - 3,8,12,20,34,52

ZAYLOR - 40

ZEIGLER - 10,39

ZENTMEYER - 44,59,60

www.ingramcontent.com/pod-product-compliance
Lightning Source LLC
Chambersburg PA
CBHW061503040426
42450CB00008B/1473